RISE
OF THE
GOOD WOLF

*Releasing our Self
into our Truth*

Kelly Pellatt

Rise of the Good Wolf

Published by Good Wolf Publishing

Originally published in 2016 by Good Wolf Publishing, Langley, Canada

Library and Archives Canada Cataloguing in Publication

Printed and Bound in the USA

ISBN-13: 978-0-9948758-0-8
ISBN-10: 0-9948758-0-0
ISBN-13: 978-0-9948758-2-2 (hc)
ISBN-13: 978-0-9948758-1-5 (epub)
ISBN-13: 978-0-9948758-3-9 (Kindle)

Cover Design by Marlow Pellatt
Cover Art ©LADYING/Shutterstock.com
Cover ©Kelly Pellatt
Printed in USA

To Natashia and Shavaun,
May the joy you bring to my life be returned to yours in
everlasting abundance!

CONTENTS

PERMISSIONS

The author thanks the following publishers and authors for permission to reprint material copyrighted or controlled by them.

Captain A.D. Chater. "Letters from the Front - The Christmas Truce." Permission graciously granted by Chater Family (S.Chater).

Tommy Douglas. "Humanity First" (Policy Speech, 1944). Used with Permission of the Douglas Coldwell Foundation.

Nelson Mandela. *Long Walk to Freedom.* Reprinted with permission of the Hachette Book Group USA Inc.

Black Elk and John G. Neihardt. *Black Elk Speaks: Being the Life Story of a Holy Man of the Oglala Sioux.* Permission granted by the University of Nebraska Press.

Chief [Luther] Standing Bear. *Land of the Spotted Eagle, New Edition.* Permission granted by the University of Nebraska Press.

PREFACE

It was towards the end of October 2013, when the chill of winter announces its presence and reminds us that hibernation season is upon us here in Canada, when the seeds of *Rise of the Good Wolf* presented themselves. The year prior, my winter project was to write a series of memoirs based on my father's stories - a legacy for his family. Listening to my father reflect upon on his life's journey - his lessons, achievements, regrets, and discoveries, it struck me that the experiences he was most proud of were the ones where he had made a positive difference in other's lives. His regrets were related to areas of his life where he felt he could have given more of himself.

By sharing our life stories, both good and bad, we open others up to reflecting upon and observing their own lives. When we can identify misguided motivation and fears we become curious about directions we would rather explore in our lives.

Internal clarity begins with locating our Truth. We can inspire others to Self- reflect but we are not in control of the deeper exploration their discoveries may take them. We are not experts on others' Truths. If I believe that another's destiny is to follow mine, then I am not walking in my Truth. Our destinies do cross paths with others, but we each have our own to follow. Mine led me to become a therapist; I believe it was my early experiences of working through adversity that opened me up to this deep interest. To make transparent the false messages we have learned and made strong can be a great battle to turn away from, but discoveries we experience as we live in our Truth make us eternally grateful that we persevered through these battles.

Early in my career I read some work by psychoanalyst D.W. Winnicott (1896 - 1971) and was introduced to his concepts of True Self and False Self.[1] Winnicott explored these two selves in depth in his work. They are generally represented as follows: Our True Self is that spontaneous, authentic, alive self, our *natural self.* The False Self is a defensive facade where we learned to seek external gratification from the approval or expectations of others; on the outside we may

[1] D.W.Winnicott, *The Maturational Processes and the Facilitating Environment: Studies in the Theory of Emotional Development* (London: The Hogarth Press and the Institute of Psycho-Analysis, 1965), 140-152.

appear to be real but on the inside we feel empty. Winnicott saw the role of the False Self as important early in life when we developed it to protect the hidden True Self from being harmed. The degree to which we nurture the False Self depends on the degree in which we needed it in our formative years growing up. I have incorporated these concepts into my language, and I present them throughout *Rise of the Good Wolf* as a frame of reference to help us locate our Truth. Winnicott left a legacy of love when he gave us these beautiful concepts to guide our Selves.

Rise of the Good Wolf began as a tribute of love to my daughters. As I began to write, I soon recognized that the threads of experience, awareness, thoughts and lessons presented throughout *Rise of the Good Wolf* came from various past and present experiences from a variety of sources. My experiences are just one thread amongst many threads that make up the whole of this book. There are many stories presented throughout this book from various eras, people, nations and ecosystems - they remind us we are all significant and necessary threads, woven together with other threads that bring us deeper into our awareness of Self. We do not arrive at the full realization of our Self by being on this journey alone - this is why *Rise of the Good Wolf* needed to be put back into the world to share, invite and ultimately expand our curiosity of Self.

The story of the Good Wolf and the Bad Wolf gives voices to the True Self and the False Self. The wolf that replenishes life energy, when we are guided by it, is our Good Wolf and represents all that is good and true; it nurtures our True Self. The Wolf that takes life energy away is the Bad Wolf and represents our fears and false messages; it nurtures our False Self. The story of the two wolves is told in Chapter One. Like many others before me, I was deeply inspired by this story which gives clarity to what can often feel confusing and overpowering in our minds. I have shared the Good Wolf story with my daughters, my friends and many of my clients I have seen over the years in therapy. Sharing our sacred stories not only helps others, but it keeps them alive in us: giving love nurtures love. Our desire to be present in the lives of others is a powerful motivator and challenges us to go deeper into our relationship with Self.

In the process of writing this book I found myself reflecting on experiences I had moved past and grown from. There was no avoiding the reality that in order to talk about Truth, I needed to talk about some of my challenging experiences that brought me deeper into my Truth. "Do you really think this would be helpful to others?" was my question to Self, and always the reply was, "Yes!" Every time I worked through a resistance, I came out free of the insecurity attached to it - a profound reminder that when we are being present in our Truth we will have continual opportunities to face fears and journey deeper into our Self and our world. The experience of writing this book has reinforced to me that as long as I remain a humble student in my life, open to learning from mistakes, remaining curious about the endless wonders of this world, and guiding myself towards these wonders, my experience on earth will be continually enriched.

PART ONE

OUR TRUE SELF, FALSE SELF, AND OUR GOOD WOLF AND BAD WOLF

CHAPTER ONE

BECOMING ACQUAINTED WITH OUR TRUTH

A loving heart is the beginning of all knowledge.
Thomas Carlyle

In our busy, fast-paced world we may believe we do not have any time for our Self - perhaps the idea of True Self may even sound foreign. The risk of losing sight of our Self is very real in a world where distractions can fill our days from morning to night. When we are in touch with the essence of our authentic, natural Self we will know why the journey through obstacles to live in this essence is worth it. If we are too busy, too angry, too fearful, and too preoccupied with measuring our worth against external factors - if we focus more on what we can get from this world rather than what we can give - we will be wandering away from our Truth. Our life will not feel balanced. If we feel too tired or too busy to do something healthy; attribute our worth to objects, images, and the belief that we are better or less than others; we will be nurturing a false truth. Anything we connect to that distracts us from living in our Truth also distracts us from celebrating the true essence of others. Thankfully, it is never too late to step into our life.

When we step back and reflect on moments in our life - carefree moments where we celebrated the most precious of life's wonders, where our whole being was wrapped up in the bliss of living - we will have located the essence of Self. Even fleeting moments where we experienced the awe of a magnificent sunset, a flying eagle overhead or the act of kindness from another - these golden experiences are gifts, they remind us where we desire to live internally. When we come back to the elements that nurture our Truth, we are reminded of why it is necessary to nourish these experiences. Life becomes clearer when we are being guided from our Truth.

If adult life means we are just managing all our roles, we will run the risk of feeling depleted. When we come back and engage our world with the curiosity of a child we will get back in touch with wonder which connects us to our world in meaningful ways. Much of our learning is finding our way back to our path. On this journey we discover our destinies.

The desire to want to help clear a path for others to follow their destiny is a testament to the potential for goodness that resides in each and every one of us if we choose to follow this path.

Helen Keller was trapped by a massive barrier. She became blind and deaf after an illness she contracted at nineteen months of age. She was born in Alabama in the year 1880. In her era there was not a lot of support for her condition, but her family persevered and found twenty-year-old Anne Sullivan. Anne was visually impaired and had been a former student of the Perkins Institute for the Blind in South Boston. Anne was patient with Helen. In spite of temper tantrums and frustrations, Anne persevered in her attempts at teaching Helen. In the second month of daily lessons where Anne would give Helen an object in one hand and in the other spell the letters of the object with her finger there was a breakthrough. Helen made the association of the motions her teacher was making on one of her hands while running her other hand under water. She understood that the motions symbolized "water." Helen became manic in her excitement of this awareness, exhausting Anne with the desire to know the names of the objects in her world.

With the support of others, Helen was enabled to break free of a massive barrier; there was no stopping the wonders she would discover. In 1904 at the age of twenty-four Helen became the first deaf blind person to earn a Bachelor's degree and went on to learn to speak and hear people by reading their lips with her hands. She wrote books and gave speeches. From the love of her family and the dedication of her teacher and lifelong friend Anne Sullivan, there was no end to Helen's possibilities.[2] We cannot underestimate the power that love and patience had in allowing Helen to open up to her life and inspire millions to do the same.

As it was for Helen, the excitement of breaking free of barriers to follow our destiny is a liberation like no other. We do not take this freedom for granted. To help others access their

---

[2] Joseph P. Lash, *Helen and Teacher: The Story of Helen Keller and Anne Sullivan Macey*. (Boston: Da Capo Press, 1997).

Truth beyond barriers is a joy like no other. For every person breaking free into the world with their Truth, many more people will be inspired to locate and nurture theirs. If we can help others clear a path to this journey we will be nurturing a culture of love. When we believe in our Self we believe in others. It is this Truth that inspired me to become a therapist and continues to bring me deeper into my destiny.

As we work through adversity and identify insecure attachments and false truths, we become aware of experiences that have touched the essence of our Truth.

When I reflect on the past, I have come to see the summer I turned nine years old as the year I became familiar with my path. I did not realize this then, but as time has gone by and I became reacquainted with elements that nurture my Truth, I have come to regard this time in my life as a time of *awakening*. I call it the "summer of the honey bees." Our family (my parents, younger brother and older sister) lived in a small two-bedroom beach cottage with a five-foot beach wall built to stop the ocean waves at high tide from claiming our land. Sunsets were magnificent, and life was in constant motion. Each day I awoke to a new wonder. We had a seagull friend we named Sam who visited us every day hoping that we would share our food with him. There were storms we retreated from but were in awe of; we shivered with excitement watching them through our cottage window. I remember how alive I felt falling to sleep with the sound of raging ocean waves. We would rush out the next morning searching the beach for washed-up treasures. With the exception of a few tragedies including the beautiful seal that washed up, killed from a gunshot to its torso, beach life was filled with endless positive adventure. We had a simple dwelling but we lived in a vast and expansive space of wonder - we were one element amongst a whole rhythm of life around us. Perhaps because our whole family was immersed in this beauty we had room to freely explore both internally and externally.

Quite naturally I became drawn to setting my Self down on our beach wall after a long day of play. I freely lost my Self in thoughts as I embraced the glory of magnificent sunsets over the water. I discovered a beehive that summer and became fascinated with the honey bee, asking questions to anyone who could help me understand them more. They worked so hard and they gave us honey. One day I dipped my finger in a honey jar then ran to the area where the bees congregated. I held my finger out, and they came landing directly onto the honey. I was elated that my plan worked so I could study them closer. When too many came, I retreated slowly until the last bee flew off. Somehow my curiosity and respect of the honey bees did not lead me to fear them. I was cautious of them, but I did not fear them; I respected them.

As I sat on my beach wall at sunset after my parley with the honey bees, digesting all the wonder I had come to learn about these marvelous little creatures, I felt compelled to give them a song. I sat on that wall well into the night until my song in honor of the honey bees was complete. I have never forgotten that song. Over the years when I experience that familiar deep connection to nature, people, the stars, moon, rivers, birds and many other beautiful wonders of this world, I remember the honey bee song and with a sense of deep gratitude I sing it.

Lots and lots of honey bees I sing in my old age,
especially the ones we used to know
Fa la la la la la
Oh, I sure do love those honey bees,
they do so much for you and me . . .
O yes I love those hooooooney beeees!
la la la la la la . . . la la la la la la . . . la la la . . . la la la la
I sure do love those hooooneeey beees!

> To be reawakened to the magic of first discoveries is to be reawakened to our Self and our world.

I remember making mud pies when I was three, and I remember the beautiful sky and the clouds forming the most amazing shapes my eyes had ever seen. I remember the magical ball that appeared in the night sky - no matter how hard I wished upon the stars to drop the glowing ball to earth, it would not come. I remember how I awoke to this wonder again by bringing my children into the natural world so they too could become lost in the world of discovery. In doing this for them, I rediscovered this wonder in me. I am still mesmerized by that magical moon in the sky and still feel that same sense of wonder when I look upon it. I have learned that when I am disconnected from this wonder I am usually too distracted by external demands and insecurities I have believed and nurtured. At these times I feel like I have let go of the hand of the person I was responsible for keeping close. This awareness reminds me to work through the distractions that took my focus away. If I lose touch with my Self then I lose touch with the most important connections to my Self.

If we attach our worth to external factors or isolate our Self to protect or avoid real or imagined fear we are most likely nurturing a False Self: a defensive facade which leaves us feeling disconnected, empty and lacking internal gratification. Our True Self - that authentic, spontaneous, alive Self - needs to be in our world exploring and discovering, learning from and working through fear.[3]

> If I am too preoccupied with my insecurities, I lose sight of the most sacred connections in my life.

There is no fog too thick to impair the light of clarity. When we move past distractions that have kept us from being accessible to our True Self we experience a happier life because we see beyond those distractions. We see that being in our world with kindness and love opens our Self up to our world and draws us closer to our Self and others.

---

[3] D.W. Winnicott, *The Maturational Processes.*

Moving Past Fears

> *You gain strength, courage and confidence by every experience in which you really stop to look fear in the face. You are able to say to yourself, "I have lived through this horror. I can take the next thing that comes along." You must do the thing you think you cannot do.*
> Eleanor Roosevelt

There are many false truths we will need to expose so we do not avoid living in our world with our Truth. For example, social media such as Facebook, cannot be a substitute for the personal connections we develop through human contact.

As we move forth in our Self journey, we will come across fears which can in some cases feel like massive and impossible barriers. It may be of some solace to know that on our journey of working through fears we discover our beautiful Self. Because we no longer desire to listen to negative messages that keep us oppressed, we face the struggle of rising above them. The freedom we experience from working through our struggles with insecurity will help to support us in the future when we face new struggles.

In my early life I believed that space for authenticity needed to be defended, that others may try from time to time try to *steal my joy* in their efforts to diminish or control me. Clearly I felt threatened by this dynamic. In defense of this fear I learned to build a strong line of defense to protect what was mine. In high school, I capitalized on my outgoing nature. On one hand being popular gave me space to be me, but on the other hand my need to be popular was motivated by insecurity. It was a defensive stance, and it was exhausting, especially when challenged.

As a young mother in my late teens I had less of a desire to invest my energy in this direction as my focus was on my children. The challenge, I now realize, was to stay focused. Much of my growth in revealing and working through insecurities has been in recognizing if I wandered too far away from where my focus needed to be I could not be available to others in the way I desired. My children were the beacons of clarity that woke me to this truth.

Unhealthy coping mechanisms - whether they be drugs, alcohol, denial, projecting and internalizing anger, jealousy, and controlling others - are ways we defend against fear. These mechanisms (our walls) block us from seeing our Truth, and they nurture our insecure False Self. They keep us separated from our Self and others. The question is: What Self do we want to bring into our world - our False Self or our True Self? Whether I am tired and grumpy or angry and upset, I will not expand in my growth if I hurt my Self and others in any way. I will not learn how to properly soothe my pain and learn from my frustrations if I avoid looking at the impact my actions have on my Self and others. The more I open up to my own learning and unlearning, the less judgmental I am.

> In the deep crevasses of my unconscious mind I have caught my False Self at play, indulging in behaviors I told my Self I do not do.

Our desire to live authentically does motivate us to dig deeper and expose the layers of false truths we have listened to and nurtured. The more curious we become about our own thoughts and how they influence our actions the less likely we will be to live with the illusion that we do not cause harm.

A few years ago I exposed negative thoughts that brought me deeper into my awareness of this truth. This lesson occurred along the bike route that I have been riding for many years. Initially I loved passing through an old family-run farm along this route. I would stop, visit the cows and savor a moment of bliss amongst this old farm. Over time I began to feel uncomfortable visiting the cows. Somehow I had shifted to feeling blissful through this area of my ride to wanting to speed through it. I felt sad seeing the cows, knowing they were going to be processed for meat. After some time I wondered about my shift in thinking. I recognized that my negative thoughts about the farm and the woman farmer I often saw when I passed through, arose because I felt guilty that I enjoyed eating beef. I recognized that this shift in my thinking had occurred at an unconscious level.

When I observed my reaction of judgment towards the farmer, I felt horrible. I knew immediately I was judging her because I had difficulty seeing my own dissociation from her way of living and where the food I ate came from. This farm was ethically run - the cows were happy, grazing freely in beautiful pasture. I did not even know where the meat I ate came from. Now when I ride past this farm, I give thanks for this lesson that brought me deeper into my Truth. Perhaps partly from guilt, but mostly from gratitude, I smile towards the farm woman when I see her; she still does not meet my gaze, but I take solace in knowing that my silent greeting is one of love, not negative judgment.

It can be extremely difficult to expose our own negative thoughts which can cause harm but if we do not learn to look upon moments of awareness as a triumph over our False Self we will limit our ability to nurture a culture of love, and we will limit our Self from the freedoms we innately desire.

I have always respected people who are honest about their struggles and are trying to overcome them. I feel they are less judgmental of others because they desire to work through the blocks that keep them from connecting to themselves and others. They give me inspiration to work through my own insecurities. I have seen beautiful people shut down by others who mistook their transparency as a weakness to be controlled or criticized. Quite contrary to being a weakness, working through insecurities helps us become more transparent to our Self and others - this is a profound strength.

There are behaviors we will come to recognize that we engage in because of our insecurities. Some are obvious and many others are not. As we work through our obvious defenses we will uncover the hidden ones to.

This past winter my dear friend's parents were visiting from Australia, and I had invited their whole family over for dinner.

Prior to eating, I warned them that I am not consistent with my gravy. I shared an observation my youngest daughter told me. She said "I have never met anyone who could be so inconsistent with their gravy - one time it could be the best gravy in the world and the next time it could be the worst." I laughed at this family joke but obviously deep down I was worried the gravy that night could lean towards bad. What touched my heart deeply was a spontaneous act of beautiful graciousness. My friend's father not only complimented me on my gravy, he poured it on his plate after his meal and raved about it as he ate his gravy soaked bun. His kindness woke me up to my own negativity towards my Self. Not everyone would respond in the same way he did.

This experience led me think about how sometimes without even realizing it, we can open our Self up to negativity. If we are negative towards our Self we give permission for others to be negative towards us too. When people respond to our negativity with a loving heart, they reflect Truth back to us. If we are listening, we will receive their gift of love. My friend's father had nurtured a loving Self and from this direction he opened me up to a deeper layer of my Truth.

We can listen to both negative and positive messages. Each

time we rise higher than a negative message, we will have removed another stone from our wall of fear. In time, this wall becomes smaller and less oppressive. We become increasingly free to live in the world with our Truth. There are many stories of wisdom throughout history that speak to our desire to rise above fear. These stories guide us towards the power of love where I believe our living is intended to be. One of my favorites is a tale about the Good Wolf and the Bad Wolf. Versions of this story are widely thought to be a Native American Cherokee legend. I contacted the Cherokee Nation in Oklahoma to verify this and was informed that this story is not Cherokee. From their research, the Cherokee Nation believed the story came from the new age movement. There are some other ideas about the origin of this story, but it is widely viewed as folklore.[4] No matter in what form I have seen it presented, the story of the Good Wolf and the Bad Wolf is beautiful. Perhaps it is a story that belongs to all of us and takes on the form in which we can best hear it.

---

[4] The story of the Good Wolf and the Bad Wolf was thought to have originated as Cherokee Folklore, although much evidence indicates more recent origins: "Origin of 'Native American' Wise Tale About 'Two Dogs'?" Google Answers, Google.com, accessed February 19, 2015, http://answers.google.com/answers/threadview?id=321024.

The Good Wolf and the Bad Wolf

A wise elder was highly revered by his people - he always seemed to guide others in a good direction. One day his grandson came to him for guidance. He was feeling angry and upset after being cheated by one of his friends. Grandfather invited him to sit down and then began to tell him the story of the Good Wolf and the Bad Wolf.

"Grandson," he said,

"Everyone has a Good Wolf and a Bad Wolf inside of them."

Meeting his Grandfather's eyes, the boy replied,

"Everyone?"

"Yes, everyone," answered Grandfather and went on to explain,

"When we feed the Good Wolf we are rewarded and replenished with life energy. Even when we face great challenges, when we follow what is right and good we will become stronger and wiser and will work towards making a difference with love, not hate."

Grandson nodded in understanding and then he asked his Grandfather how he could see his Bad Wolf.

Grandfather explained,

"When we feed the Bad Wolf we give life energy away but it is not replenished. Sometimes we give our self over to our challenges and learn to hate our self and others. This energy can lead to other destructive forces such as jealousy and revenge. It closes us off to the life replenishing wonders in our world. The Bad Wolf is always hungry but never satisfied. The Bad Wolf takes life energy but does not give back life energy."

Grandson thought about the Bad Wolf and the Good Wolf and could see both in himself - but he remained confused. He could not think of a time he saw the Bad Wolf in his beloved Grandfather and asked,

"Grandfather, do you have a Bad Wolf inside of you?"

Grandfather looked deeply into the eyes of his Grandson, allowing their spirits to connect and said,

"Yes - I do; I battle it every day."

Still confused, Grandson asked,

"Which wolf is stronger?"

Grandfather smiled lovingly and said,

"Dear grandson, the answer is simple: the stronger wolf is the one we choose to feed."

Working Through Resistances

It is not the end of the physical body that should worry us. Rather, our concern must be to live while we're alive - to release our inner selves from the spiritual death that comes with living behind a facade designed to conform to external definitions of who and what we are.
Elizabeth Kübler-Ross

As we continue to guide our Self with our Good Wolf, our

Bad Wolf may rebel; we may experience a great struggle from within as our fear messages become aroused. When we hold tight and continue to nurture our Truth, we will begin to rise above our fears and discover an ever-expanding, beautiful Self as we seek healthier connections to attach to in our world.

We may discover that for too long we allowed our Good Wolf to be corralled by fear of Bad Wolves. Our desire to be out in our world discovering new experience and nurturing healthier messages challenges false beliefs and negative messages that we cannot survive in our world. When we stop listening to messages that keep us trapped in fear, we face these fears with a new message. Looking directly towards our False Self we say,

"No. This is not my Truth."

With this clarity, we turn our focus towards our Good Wolf. We will feel the depth of excitement and gratitude as we continually greet the Wolf that nurtures the true essence of our being.

In time, we discover the Bad Wolf is no longer the strongest focus of our lives. We no longer live in the illusion that we need to nurture the Bad Wolf to survive. There will be battles. When the Bad Wolf rises, we will know there is more we need to learn.

> Our Good Wolf has always stood with our goodness, even when we have not. With this knowing, our allegiance to this Wolf becomes strong.

The more we listen for our internal Truth, the less we will desire to be caught up in false messages because we are better able to recognize them: Why am I saying yes when I want to say no? Why am I taking my stress out on my family? Why am I lying about myself? Why am I allowing my Self to be used by this person - what am I afraid of? Why am I being so controlling - what am I afraid of?

Our strongest reactions and resistances to change usually reflect our greatest fears. Our fear messages emerged through various experiences throughout our lives and gained strength each time we nurtured them. The person we *learned to be,* we now recognize, is in conflict with *who we actually are.* When we become aware of our fears, avoidances and insecurities we have an opportunity to replace unhealthy behaviors with healthier ones. If we feel, for example, that we can only start something new if we have someone else to do this with us, then we have identified a fear. As we continue to listen to the Good Wolf we will find it harder to listen to rationalizing thoughts of why we *shouldn't work towards something that is good for us*. In time we will come to see such battles as opportunities to work through resistance that will bring us deeper into our Truth and deeper into our life.

Guiding Self With Truth

> *All truths are easy to understand once they are discovered;*
> *the point is to discover them.*
> Galileo Galilei

When they have been nurtured a long time, our deepest insecurities can mask themselves as truths. Any message we give our Self or others that demeans goodness is a *false truth*.

As we continue to observe our false truths, we will reveal deeper layers of fear. We may come to see that we are *afraid of the unknown* and instead of moving forward through uncharted territory, we fall back to something that has become familiar but not good for us or others. For example, instead of seeking new and healthier connections, we may wish for others to be different so we can feel better. We may observe our insecure False Self ruminating on questions we have no control over: Why can't she understand? How can he do what he is doing? Can't she see what she is doing is so selfish? When we understand that feeding such thoughts is destructive to our Self and others we are more likely to motivate our Self to work through our fear. If we are resentful towards others and do not work toward resolution of this negative emotion, we will be at risk of routinely undermining our own and others happiness.

As we nurture our Good Wolf and dance in the space we have freed from our insecurities, our happiness may elicit envy in others. Pure happiness is a state of mind, not a commodity we use to make others feel bad. This is why it can come as such a shock when our own happy state of mind is interrupted by an act of envy, selfishness or control from another - yet no one can steal our joy.

In the classic Grimm's Brothers fairy tale, *Cinderella*, written over two hundred years ago, a beautiful maiden with a kind and gentle heart is the focus of envy. Through demoralization and deprivation, Cinderella's stepmother and stepsisters became ugly in their antics to oppress Cinderella. In spite of this, Cinderella's spirit could not be broken. Although no living person gave her love - she found love in the beauty of nature and animals. She kept her deceased mother close to her heart, never forgetting to nurture the words her mother left with her, "dear child, be good and pious." As Cinderella grew, her desire to explore her world grew as well. She learned of a royal ball where all the maidens of the village were invited for a chance to win the heart of the kind prince. No matter how hard she bargained, pleaded and appealed, Cinderella was forbidden to go.

With the will of her heart and the goodness she attached to in her world, she found a way to escape her oppression and follow her destiny. Her inner beauty was highlighted in a dress that caught the Prince's attention, but it was her True Self he fell in love with. With elements of fear still resounding in her, Cinderella went to the ball but fled back home before the eager prince could learn more about her. In her haste she left one of her golden shoes behind. The prince came in search of his true love announcing he would marry the maiden whose foot fit the golden shoe. In desperation to force their feet into the golden shoe, one stepsister cut off her toe and the other her heel. This did not fool the prince, and he inquired if there were other maidens living within the home, to which Cinderella's father replied "only the little stunted kitchen-wench which my late wife left behind."[5] This did not deter the prince and much to the horror of her stepmother and sisters, he insisted that the hidden maid be called. Cinderella calmly washed her face and hands, then entered the room and set herself on a wooden stool. She pulled off her wooden shoe and gently slipped on the golden slipper. The Prince recognized her immediately and they rode off together.

Cinderella knew she deserved happiness. To be good and pious does not mean that we accept cruelty. Cinderella was not rescued. She worked through her oppression to bring her Self into the world. The Prince was good and saw her true beauty underneath the golden dress. But first Cinderella needed to bring herself into the world to be seen. If we take fairy tales literally we may miss the moral lessons in them. When we connect to someone with whom we have mutual regard for the True Self, we have connected with true love and this is a blessing. Envy of the true beauty in others is ugly, and when nurtured it is destructive and oppressive. It does not nurture a culture of love.

---

[5] Jacob Grimm and Willhem Grimm, "Cinderella," in *Grimm's Complete Fairy Tales* (San Diego: Canterbury Classics, 2011) 86.

Although Bad Wolf projections can be extremely uncomfortable to deal with (especially if they bring up historical pain), they are not ours to keep. We do need to walk very close to our Good Wolf when we are being challenged to remind our Self not to be pulled in a direction that is not healthy for us. The stronger the challenge, the deeper we must go into our Truth. When we nurture our Good Wolf, our world opens up in profound ways. When the thought of causing harm to our Self and others becomes more intolerable than being controlled by our false messages and fears, we are listening to our well nurtured Truth.

Nurturing Trust With Truth

I've learned that people will forget what you said, people will forget what you did, but people will never forget how you made them feel.
Maya Angelou

Recognizing the process of our own journey does help us to be mindful of other's journeys of growth. If we prevent others from growing with us, we prevent our Self from growing with them. When we are open to learning from our mistakes we will be open to others learning from theirs. This openness builds relationships of trust which allow us to be more transparent, patient and forgiving with each other as we work towards the mutual goal of growth.

I am reminded of a time when my youngest daughter was fifteen; we were driving together and having a conversation that reflected her maturing conscience. I knew it was important to keep the environment open, and I listened intently to what she had to say. After some time she turned to me and said,

"Mom, I was reading my old diary and I can't believe the mean things I said about you in it; I felt so bad I ripped the pages out."

She was thirteen and fourteen when she wrote these entries. Mostly I learned she was angry with limitations I had imposed on her freedom, which she was now recognizing were reasonable. I felt so proud of her - not because she ripped the pages out of her diary but because she felt enough trust in me that she could express her Self in this way. Her confession led to an open discussion about the power of emotions and need to guide our Self with patience when we face our triggers.

With a heart full of love I felt compelled to validate her experience by explaining I did the same thing when I was a young girl, and like her I did not like reading the angry words I had written. We engaged in an open dialogue about learning from our mistakes and the importance of forgiving our Self and others.

I truly believe it is this kind of trust that brings us deeper into our relationships. If I had taken my daughter's confession personally, I would have shut her down and she would not have felt safe to open up to me in the way she did. I was reminded that if I was going to be effective in helping my daughters through their teen years I needed to nurture patience in myself and encourage honest communication with them. I became a better parent of teenage girls after that conversation.

In most relationships we work through some level of adversity and often become closer and more respectful of each other through this process. Sometimes, in spite of our best intentions, we may find ourselves in relationships that repeatedly undermine our happiness; in this case we need to look concertedly for a new direction. These can be times when our trust in Truth and goodness is our only beacon of light we must follow as we navigate through great storms.

> In spite of how strong some of our fears may be, our True
> Self does not want to be defined or controlled by fear.

When our motivations are born of love, we step out of the
individual idea of Self and into our world. From this truth we
see our Self and others as equally deserving of love,
encouragement, success and joy. When we live in our world
with this truth we will be nurturing a culture of love. We will
know that people and resources are not placed on this earth
for the benefit of our individual needs. We will know that we
are visitors for a short time sharing our world with many other
organisms whom are also here for a short time contributing to
a continuum of life. If we disrupt this continuum, we disrupt
destinies.

A society grows great when old men plant trees whose
shade they know they shall never sit in.
Greek proverb

CHAPTER TWO

OUR TRUE SELF
GARDEN

Though I do not believe that a plant will spring up where no seed has been, I have great faith in a seed. Convince me that you have a seed there, and I am prepared to expect wonders.

Henry David Thoreau

Our structured world can be an extremely distracting place. Unless we engage in a regular practice of *stepping back* to our own place of reflection, we may become too caught up in the continuous events of our life and too responsive to the stimuli they provoke. If we feel we have no time for our Self, this is a good indication we need to create time for our Self. Whether we choose to walk, meditate, pray, practice yoga, play sports, read or write, what we do in our free time will depend on what we feel we need. As we continue to nurture our Self in this way we come to better know our Self through increased clarity. I have come to identify this space we create to nurture our Self as our *True Self Garden.*

With a nurtured True Self we are better able to maneuver our way through obstacles without losing sight of our Truth. No matter how beautiful our surroundings, if we are not present and embracing this beauty, we are not connecting to it. I was reminded of this recently when I was out for a bike ride. I rode past a woman who was power walking on the path in front of me. It was a beautiful spring day with amazing scenery and life swarming around us, but it was apparent the woman was not noticing this beauty. She was marching forward involved in a loud and agitated conversation with someone on her mobile phone. One hour later on my return, I passed her again and again she was involved in a tense conversation on her phone. Perhaps this is what she needed to be doing that day, but she did remind me of how we can miss out on so much beauty when we are preoccupied.

No matter how tranquil, spiritual and enlightening the environment that surrounds us may be, if we are not leaving our distractions behind, we will not embrace the peace in our surroundings and nurture calm in our Self.

We cannot avoid being with our Self; the more we avoid, the greater our internal struggle will be. Sometimes, when we can no longer tolerate internal weeds in the garden of our life, we begin to look at our life in deeper ways. False messages are weeds - clutter in our True Self garden. If we believe that "others are better and more deserving than us" or that "we are better and more deserving than others" then we are most likely listening to false messages. We cannot deal with these false message weeds if we avoid them. When we step back into our Self and weed attentively in our garden, we forge paths that will guide us deeper into our Truth. Underneath the weeds are beautiful seeds that are desperate to grow.

As we continue to cultivate our garden, we nurture a deeper respect for the sacredness of this space. We will see and experience the wonders that exist here and will be reminded of this wonder when we move about in our world collecting new wonders to bring back to our garden. With this knowing, we will tread lightly when we are invited into the sacred space of others. For each garden is as sacred as another with its own variety of flowers to be treasured. When we bring negativity into another's life we bring them weeds and trample their beautiful flowers.

Cultivating Our Garden

Even the richest soil, if left uncultivated will produce the rankest weeds.
Leonardo da Vinci

What we forage for in our world will reflect what we nurture. If we have taken or demanded what others have worked hard to cultivate, that beautiful plant we took from someone else's garden may become a weed in ours. Taking is not a reliable source of nutrients for our garden. If we use others to feed our greed, we will find these sources will dry up either through nutrient depletion or others closing their gates to us. We can search for new sources to deplete or come back to our own garden and nurture Truth that connects us to our Self and our world with love.

If we are fortunate to be offered a cutting of a beautiful plant we have admired in another's garden and receive this gift with love - not expectation - it will thrive in our garden. When we see how a simple act of pure kindness can open our life up to this goodness we share with others, we will have an idea of what kind of energy we want to nurture in this world. There are no exceptions or justifications to treating others disrespectfully. Others do not owe us anything. Whether people are rich or poor, popular or unpopular, famous or not famous, compromised or not, there are no justifications to cause them harm.

Memories of times in my life where I have fed my Bad Wolf and nurtured weeds come up from time to time and remind me of which wolf I want to feed. When I was around twenty-one years old, I was attending college and rode public transit to and from school. This was a time of discovery. I was taking everything in and found these rides to be quite enjoyable. I loved being amongst the rhythms of others' lives. One day while on my way home, a young man came onto the bus. He carried what seemed to be a large package under his coat and purposefully proceeded to the back of the crowded bus and squeezed in beside me. Slowly he revealed what he was hiding. It was a small cage full of gerbils. There must have been at least ten of these tiny creatures scurrying around. Instantly I became curious, and we struck up a conversation.

He told me that he was transporting his pets over to his girlfriend's house to breed with her gerbils. He was enthusiastic about his little friends and the gerbil business he was starting up.

I was happy to be engaged in this conversation. I was aware of others around me snickering, but I did not pay too much attention to this. In retrospect I truly believe my authentic interest in this young man's love of gerbils did help him not to be concerned about the judgments of others; but then an incident happened, and it all changed. The bus made a sudden stop and everyone lurched forward, including the gerbils. The cage flew out of the young man's arms and crashed onto the floor. The roof fell off and most of the terrified gerbils escaped. Frantically the man crawled on the bus floor calling for his gerbils by their names. Laughter from the people at the back of the bus was loud. One by one he would locate each animal and put it back into the safety of the cage.

The gerbils that were not found made their way towards the front of the bus where people were not aware of them. Every time the young man heard a scream he lurched up from the ground and began to search the area where the sound of terror came from. He had one objective: to find his pets and bring them back to safety. He was the only one searching; the rest of us at the back were rolling around in fits of laughter. When all his pets were back in their cage, the man retreated to his seat and stared directly ahead at nothing in particular. He had shut everyone else in the bus out. I saw he looked both angry and sad. The back of the bus fell silent; I felt smaller than his tiniest pet. I could not take back the fun I had at this poor man's expense. He had trusted me, and I had let him down. I caused this man injury. I could have gone to the floor and helped him; later we could have laughed together about the whole ordeal; the outcome would have been different. I recognized later that my behavior could have affirmed a false truth for this young man: that people are cruel and not to be trusted. This was not the kind of truth I wanted to nurture. I forgave myself and have made a conscious effort to carry this lesson with me.

Injuries from others that we have endured and internalized in our lives can be the most difficult weeds to deal with. It can be our strongest challenge to rise above the wounds from these injuries, but they are also the most valuable and empowering experiences we can use for growth. They inform us of the impacts our actions have on others. In cultivating weeds, we reclaim space that was rightfully ours, and that feels pretty good. If we are to expand in our growth we cannot stay locked in our garden afraid of weeds. We learn by being in our world collecting seeds - some thrive in our garden and some do not. I hope this man I met so many years ago did not stop foraging for seeds because of the weeds he came across. Our True Self does not desire to be controlled by negative forces that come from our own or others' actions. No one can destroy our beauty; only we have the ability to do that when we accept something that is not healthy for us.

Coming Back to Our Garden

I went to the woods because I wished to live deliberately, to front only the essential facts of life, and see if I could not learn what it had to teach, and not, when I came to die, discover that I had not lived.

Henry David Thoreau

When we feel angry, sad, insecure, jealous, or any other negative emotion, an important question to think about is: Why would I not want to pull my Self away to a calm place to collect my thoughts and later decide what I need to do? The harder it feels to pull our Self away from unhealthy behaviors, thoughts and patterns, the harder we must step back and look for healthier attachments to nurture our Self. This act takes power away from our Bad Wolf. Each successful step back in the direction of our Truth is a triumph for our Self. There are times I know I need to step away from my busy life because I feel too caught up in it. When the internal chatter in my mind is full of thoughts that tell me why I cannot pull my Self away, it is usually because I am in need of being pulled away. When I recognize internal chatter such as What if someone breaks into the house? Who is going to cover my work when I am gone? I am too tired to go for a bike ride - then I know I have wandered too far away from my Self and need to pull my Self in the opposite direction of these thoughts. If the battle is really strong then I most likely need to go on what I have come to know as a *True Self Pilgrimage* - a purposeful time away to nurture Self.

For me, the destination of my pilgrimage is often in nature; a place to slow down and absorb the wonders around me. This is where I can come back to being in touch with my Self. Sometimes I have gone alone on these pilgrimages, but often I go with my husband. Thankfully he enjoys replenishing himself in nature too. Once or twice a year we manage to get away for extended road trips. We have fun discovering less travelled routes. With each new discovery I find my Self being drawn out of my mind and into being present in the world around me. The internal transition from busy mind to peaceful mind usually takes a few days. When we are not off discovering something interesting, we are usually in a silent car taking in the beauty around us. We stop in town centers only to replenish food and touch base with loved ones in random coffee shops that provide internet service; then we are on our way selecting the less travelled routes back into the countryside towards our next adventure. We usually have a few destinations in mind, but we like to give ourselves plenty of time to discover new places to camp along the way. I come home from these pilgrimages feeling replenished and am reminded of the meaningful things I desire to connect to and nurture as I re- enter my busy life.

Although not as immersive as a pilgrimage, regular connections to nature remind me of the clarity I discover and rediscover on my pilgrimages and help me to keep my life in balance. When I struggle with balancing my life, it is generally time for another pilgrimage.

When we navigate in our world in the direction of our Truth, we will experience continuous clarity. We will come to recognize that the insecurities that we once feared, denied and defended actually inform us of something we need to address and deal with; our desire to move beyond them will guide us deeper into our Self. The deeper we journey into our Truth, we will recognize there is nothing on the outside that can control what is known from within. If we think there is, then we have some weeds to dig out.

Because we have nurtured experiences that inform us about how we feel when we are centered with Self, we will be better informed when we are feeling imbalanced and what we need to do bring our Self back to balance.

Being Our Self

> *With an eye made quiet by the power of harmony, and the deep power of joy, we see into the life of things.*
> William Wordsworth

I believe I caused my Self some harm when I was a young woman in my transition from carefree teenager to mother when I nurtured my fears. My husband and I were living in British Columbia's Okanagan, which is about a six-hour drive to the lower mainland metropolis of Vancouver in the same province. I had moved with him from the Vancouver area when I was six months pregnant. We had left adolescence behind in the city, and we made two babies in two years. He attended college during this time, and we returned to the big city as two very young parents focused on building a life for our little family. We settled into family residence on the campus of a major university so he could finish his education. I had some adjusting to do.

Socially I felt awkward and not sure of my Self. I allowed my Self to flow into the first people who embraced me, and this made me feel even more insecure. At one of the gatherings I was invited to, I accidentally bumped into a picture on the wall and watched helplessly as it came crashing to the ground. I felt devastated. I already felt insecure around these people, and this accident compounded the catastrophe. I apologized profusely as I cleaned up the mess and offered to have the frame repaired. Instead of being forgiven, I was berated and told how special the picture was; the hostess' father had it custom-framed for her. Somehow I stopped feeling devastated, and my mind came back to Self. It was as though my Good Wolf had been ready for this opportunity for me to see what I had ignored. I observed others around me interested in what was going on, but in a way of amusement not empathy. I suddenly felt stronger. I will never forget the clarity of the question that emerged from deep within, much louder than the predicament I was in.

"Why am I allowing my Self to be around this negative energy?"

I left that party feeling empowered and clear. I was not angry or sad. I just knew that I had been moving in a direction I did not want for my life, and I felt grateful for this awareness. Instead, I turned my attention towards the positive connections I had made.

There was another major event in my transition into listening for my Truth which occurred around the same time as the crashing picture incident so long ago. I became very ill. I was literally being choked from the inside. I could not keep out of the bathroom and became anxious to be too far away from a toilet. I was already skinny, and I began to drop weight fast. My skin turned a pale shade of white, and my energy became severely depleted. I was sent for blood work and then to a specialist because my white blood count was exceptionally high. After further tests I was diagnosed with ulcerative colitis. I was instructed by my specialist to change my diet and reduce my stress. I had a very good idea about where I could start. I needed to listen to my Truth.

I drifted away from the people I was forcing my insecure Self to be around, and moved toward the people and interests that resonated with my Truth. Most had young children just like me and also desired to live their life inclusively with them. Within months, my colitis symptoms went away and have never been back. My life began to expand in many ways. I became more aware of the insecure feeling I experience when I connect to others with a false truth; this feeling reminds me to step back and reevaluate what I need to work through as I redirect my focus towards positive attachments in my life.

I have always felt a deep sense of gratitude for the beautiful people I met at this time in my life. Their unconditional regard for me helped me to step back into my life and led me to a deep appreciation for the goodness in others. With space freed up, I began to reflect on my interests and my desire to go back to school intensified. I listened to this, and more seeds were nurtured. My husband and I continued to grow deeper into our relationship as we supported each other in school and later our career endeavors.

About two years after the colitis diagnosis, I was in a

sociology class when a profound and marvelous event happened. The professor who taught this class had an open and authentic way of relating, and I connected to this. One day a fellow student asked him how he came to study in his field of sociology. He freely explained that prior to Sociology he studied medicine because this is what his father wanted him to do. As the years went on he became increasingly resistant to his chosen career path because he wanted to study Sociology. He stayed a little longer in medicine until he became very ill with colitis. Finally he took a stand for his life, quit medicine, switched to sociology and allowed his father to work through his own disappointment. The professor said he experienced an immense relief, and within months his colitis cleared and had not returned. I felt an explosion of joy, my whole body was shaking with excitement. I wanted to jump up and down in that classroom and shout "I had the same thing happen to me!" Even though I celebrated silently, I never forgot the power of the professor's honesty, and in honor of it I share his story.

Difficult experiences we work through and gain clarity from can inform us in many profound ways. For one, they inform us of the importance of intent. We all make mistakes and can do our most profound learning from these mistakes. When we treat others mistakes personally (as though it was their intent to cause us harm) we will feed our Bad Wolf and disregard their Truth: that they were not intending to cause harm.

Several years after the crashing picture incident I was sitting on my living floor fixing a wooden frame of an antique mirror. I had placed the mirror on the floor beside me while I worked on the frame. The kids were playing with their friends in other areas of the house, and all was well until my youngest daughter's friend came bounding through the living room. Before I could get my first word out, she sprang and landed directly on top of the glass and shattered it. She leapt off as quickly as she had landed and turned around with a look of shock. I first assessed her feet which were miraculously fine, and then I saw the expression of devastation on her face when she saw what she had done. She stood frozen staring down at the shattered glass. My heart filled with empathy as I knew she felt horrible. The broken antique mirror seemed trivial compared to the need to assure her that what happened was an accident.

> When we cause our Self or others harm we choke our garden with weeds.

It is far more devastating to be a contributor to a broken spirit than it is to accept the loss of a broken object. Working through adversity in our life does open us up to deeper observations in our relations with others. How we respond to situations can have a lasting effect on others. Situations, like the one involving my daughter's friend where we are faced with a choice of responding with our Good Wolf or our Bad Wolf, make me thankful for previous experiences that opened me up to what is really important in life - to not cause harm.

Foraging in Our World

Be careful what you water your dreams with. Water them with worry and fear and you will produce weeds that choke the life from your dream. Water them with optimism and solutions and you will cultivate success.
Lao Tzu

Our True Self needs a well-balanced diet. In addition to good nutrition, we need positive connection to others, inspiration, spirituality, challenges, work, physical activities, hobbies, and rest. When we recognize imbalance in any of these areas, it is our job to listen and seek whatever it is we feel we need. How and what we do relates directly to who we are and what we need at any point in time throughout our lives. When we identify barriers to our essential needs we will have accessed clarity on what we will need to work through and forage for in our world.

I have learned a great deal about my Self through my challenges. Most profoundly I learned that if I do not step back and reflect upon my challenges, I will miss the lesson I am to learn. Much like the great pollinators in our world, we are meant to seek life nourishment and give back life nourishment. If we are too distracted by a few events in our life, we will deprive our Self and others of nutrients we need to thrive.

> We cannot be fully nourished and give back nourishment when we feed from just one flower patch.

Our lessons are all around us. In all the wonder that is life there is great lessons to learn which bring us deeper into our Truth.

A couple of years ago on a beautiful sunny spring day I asked a good friend whom I also work with if she would like to go for a walk at lunch. She agreed. The hour went quickly and, pressed for time, I bought a slice of pizza to eat on our walk back to the office. I was startled by a scraping sensation on my head and looked up just in time to catch the culprit land on a wire behind me. It was a crow. No sooner did I turn around and there was another crow directly in front of me. He also swooped down and scraped my head with his claws. As he approached the wire behind me the first crow lifted off and came at me. These clever little rascals had created a tag team method of intimidation. They seemed to be having fun at my expense. I held my pizza tight and shouted at them to go away. My reaction seemed to excite them more provoking the first crow to launch and dart my way. In an effort to appear larger and scarier than these little hooligans I began swinging my left arm into the air while maintaining a grip on the pizza in my other hand. I shouted louder:

"You're not getting my pizza - go away!"

I could see my efforts at intimidation were futile and I turned my attention towards an escape route. As soon as I saw a clearing in the road, I ran with my friend across the street towards the building we work in. I did not let go of the pizza. After we caught our breath, we turned and saw the crows had stayed behind an invisible line. Contrary to looking defeated they glared across the way at us with their chests proudly puffed. I think they did accomplish what they set out to do.

Several months later I observed what appeared to be the same crows harassing an old bald eagle who has soared, from time to time, outside my eleventh-floor office window ever since I arrived ten years before. The tag team crow duo must have been bored that day. I immediately felt they were the same little rascals that had harassed me. This was evident by the way they were taunting the old eagle. One held back while the other flew towards the eagle. When the harassing crow retreated after his plunge into the eagle, the other charged and this repeated. Generally eagles respond to pesky crows by flying at record speed in an effort to get away from them. This response excites the crows, and they send out the news to their friends that "the game is on." Crows who are in the vicinity come from all directions to play a game of "Chase the Eagle".

This old eagle did not engage in the game. He continued to soar in a circle over the landscape below where he foraged for food. When one of the duo came into contact, the eagle just flicked his massive wing as though he was swatting a fly off of his shoulder. I observed the eagle soared higher with each new circle. He was focused and was not going to be distracted from his task. Eventually the crows became bored and left. The eagle remained at a high altitude for a while longer and then with each circle began his slow descent back to the altitude he preferred for foraging. I thanked the old eagle for this important lesson to stay attentive to my life and not be so easily diverted with distractions.

Regardless of how far we have travelled on a wrong path, it is never too late to turn around. Each step we take in the direction of Self we reveal new weeds that had established in our absence. As we remain attentive on our garden path we continually nurture seeds we have freed from the weeds. This purging of false messages and fears allows us to move more fluidly in our world. As we continue to be attentive to our life in this way, we become familiar with feelings that inform us whether or not we are walking on the path of our Truth. Our great struggles are not easy. However, we will eventually see that they are experiences that provide us with some of our most profound learning. Because we have freed our Self from fear and false messages that bound us to a restricted world we become wiser to these distractions that we once attached to. When we face new fear we will know the wolf we want to call upon and walk with.

"No" is the answer from deep within.

"No" is the call from our Good Wolf,

"We will not hand our life over to fear."

"We will not hand our power over to the Bad Wolf; my garden will not be its playground."

CHAPTER THREE

RISING ABOVE ADVERSITY

We could never learn to be brave and patient if there were only joy in the world.
Helen Keller

If we feel depleted of internal resources and strength to enjoy life, we are amidst adversity which is most likely compounded by an oppressive internal dialogue: Why should I bother? This is too much for me. I cannot go on living like this. Why did this happen to me? What have I done to deserve this?

> The deeper the adversity, the deeper we must journey into our Self to rise above it.

We may ignore our Truth in place of stress, insecurity, pain, anger, and false truths because our attachment to events that make us feel this way have become strong; they have become weeds in our garden which have been nurtured. Our Truth lies beyond our fears and pain. When we recognize that we are stuck in oppressive thoughts that keep us from our True Self and others in loving ways, we have stepped back into our garden and can begin to nurture healthier messages and actions.

> Our healing brings us closer to our Self and to others.

Rising With Truth

> *There are many truths of which the full meaning cannot be realized until personal experience has brought it home.*
> John Stuart Mill

I see beautiful people come to therapy to work through

adversity. As they rise with their Truth, the desire to help others tends to rise too. This never ceases to amaze me. The need to connect in meaningful ways seems to increase when we move closer to the essence of who we are.

Stories of healing inspire us because they shine light on Truth and give us hope that we too can survive the most trying of times.

When our heart is motivated from love, it is this love we are beholden to. Betraying or turning our back on this Truth is just not an option; for when we do, we will find our Self cut off from an essential life source. Nothing is worth this cost.

When Hawaii's last Queen, Lili'uokalani accepted her position to the throne in the year 1891 after her brother, King Kalākaua's death, she was very much aware of the desperate state of affairs for native Hawaiians. She was driven by a strong sense of allegiance to her people and her beloved Hawaii. She believed in Truth. It was from this energy that she drew strength in the face of great injustice and cruelty towards her and the indigenous Hawaiian people. Her book, *Hawai'i's Story by Hawai'i's Queen,* was published in 1898; it is an incredible labor of love and holds within its pages an immense amount of wisdom from a woman who clearly could not and would not be swayed from Truth.[6] Inspired by love and the plight of her people, her book is an eternal gift of history and hope; it beckons for the core of Truth to rise above adversity.

Lili'uokalani had the innate awareness that Truth does not always prevail in the immediate future. Sometimes it can take several generations for Truth to be realized in the face of great adversity and change. Her book encompasses this wisdom. She knew her people would need great strength in the face of great oppression. She worked tirelessly to document her people's history both before and after colonization by the United States of America, lest it be forgotten; she also gave to them the gift of songs. She had written four Hawaiian national anthems in her life and many more songs. A few of her most popular, including the timeless "Aloha 'Oe" (Farewell to Thee), were written when she was jailed for treason in her own palace. When I finished reading Lili'uokalani's work of love, *Hawai'i's Story by Hawai'I's Queen,* I found myself thinking about so many beautiful and courageous people in our world who have selflessly made it their life's work to better the lives

---

[6] Liliuokalani, *Hawaii's Story By Hawaii's Queen* (1898, repr., Honolulu: Mutual Publishing, 1990).

of others. In light of injustice and selfishness there are those who stand up and work for the goodness of all - often risking their life for this cause. They are Good Wolves who keep the flame of Truth lit for the next generation. In honor of these beautiful people I wrote this letter of thanks:

Thank you Lili'uokalani for your legacy of love. You held tight to goodness no matter how great the adversity faced. Your Truth is an eternal gift. Lili'uokalani - like so many others before and after you, even when accused, tried and convicted of fabricated stories designed to shame and discredit you for the selfish gains of others - you never let go of Truth. You never let go of seeing the goodness in others. Even though bullied by powerful people from a powerful country, with each escalation of injustice you gained strength. In the face of great and powerful injustice you went deeper into your wisdom. You used your worldly tools of education to pour your heart and soul into written words for all time to ensure that Truth would never be lost. My written words only touch the essence of the deep gratitude I feel for the beautiful legacy of love you left. Your perseverance and sacrifices for Truth were not in vain.

A powerful moment that resonated strongly with Lili'uokalani and gave her immense strength occurred during an experience in court. The courtroom was packed with sympathizers for the U.S. cause. The energy was profoundly negative towards Lili'uokalani. She kept thoughts of her people in her mind, and this was the strength she drew upon. She was accused of being cold and unfeeling because her oppressors could not break her spirit. There was someone in that courtroom that did draw her attention. A kind woman whom Lili'uokalani had known to be the wife of an American lieutenant had regularly attended the trial. Later, when Lili'uokalani was sentenced for treason and jailed in her palace, she was to see this kindly courtroom visitor again.

While Lili'uokalani was watching the disrespectful sight of a group of men from a steamship practicing their drills on a church wall and graveyard across from her palace, a woman with a veil walked up and stood under the window of the room in the right hand corner of the second floor, where Lili'uokalani was jailed in her palace. She looked towards Lili'uokalani, kissed her hands to her and stood there for at least ten minutes. Just before she turned to leave, the woman lifted her veil and revealed herself to be the faithful woman who attended Liliuokalani's trial. As Liliuokalani stood gazing down upon her beautiful visitor, tears began rolling down the woman's cheeks and made their way to Lili'uokalani's heart. Emily Dickinson's beautiful words reminded me of the Good Wolf energy of this woman:

If I can stop one heart from breaking,
I shall not live in vain;
If I can ease one life the aching,
Or cool one pain,
Or help one fainting robin
Unto his nest again,
I shall not live in vain.
Emily Dickinson[7]

Moving Our Self Forward

I do not believe that sheer suffering teaches. If suffering alone taught, all the world would be wise, since everyone suffers. To suffering must be added mourning, understanding, patience, love, openness, and the willingness to remain vulnerable.

Anne Morrow Lindbergh

---

[7] Emily Dickinson, *The Complete Poems* (1924; Bartleby.com, 2000), Part I, VI, accessed June 22, 2015, www.bartleby.com/113/1006.html.

When we observe our struggles through moments of Self-reflection, we gain clarity. We need to be patient as it takes time to heal and work through adversity. A deep wound does not heal in one day. But each step we take forward is a step deeper into our Truth. We can move through our fears and insecurities and enhance our life; we can forgive our Selves and others; we do not need others approval to affirm our Truth; we can stand up to the Bad Wolf.

With each obstacle we work through, another truth will be discovered. In time, we will come to know how we feel when we need to step back and explore different possibilities. The less we resist this process, the less we will fear change. Our journey of discovery is never over, and this is a wonderful thing. As long as we are living, we will be discovering and growing. Even when we feel we have explored our paths thoroughly and can retire to a long rest, we will find that, if we rest too long, complacency will set in and we will feel this in negative ways. Our life is in constant motion. We will have many events going on around us that we are not in control of. Time is wasted when we hold onto negativity and attach our Self to dynamics that take us away from being with others in meaningful ways. Life is precious and it is meant to be celebrated. When we try to control life or become too distracted with negative events in our life we miss opportunities to embrace it.

> If we have foraged all we can on one path, it is time to discover a new one

A few years ago, while rummaging through a pile of used books at my aunt's place, I found a little book with a simple seashell on the front called *Gift from the Sea.*[8] I had found a gem. This little book took me a long time to read. I savored each sentence, and my desire to learn more about the author grew with each page. She spoke to the essence of Self in a way that reflected a woman who had navigated through great obstacles and gained clarity in the natural simplicity of life. She understood the importance of nurturing Self. The author is Anne Morrow Lindbergh (June 22, 1906 - February 7, 2001); she was a writer, mother and along with her husband Charles Lindbergh, a famous American aviator. Her first child, Charles Lindbergh Jr., was just twenty months old when he was kidnapped for ransom and found murdered in 1932. Anne Morrow rose from this tragedy, raised five children and wrote several insightful books. For Anne, the sea inspired and

---

[8] Anne Morrow Lindbergh, *Gift from the Sea: 50th Anniversary Edition* (New York: Pantheon Books, 2005).

rejuvenated. One year, in the mid-1950s, she went alone to a small beach cottage where she wrote about her reflections on life. *Gift from the Sea* is a gift Anne gave the world. She especially focused on the busy lives of women and her observations that if women do not make a conscious effort to nurture themselves through quiet moments of reflection they will run the risk of becoming lost in the demands of their lives. She advocated simplicity and being authentic. The voice of the Good Wolf resonates strongly throughout *Gift from the Sea*; it is no wonder this book written so long ago continues to impact people with its timeless wisdom.

When we listen for our Truth, we will be better able to listen for the Truth in others. There were times in my life where people believed in me, even when I did not believe in my Self. This helped me to see my Self and believe in possibilities. These experiences were essential lessons in understanding that we all have potential to be explored. On the contrary, if we shut our own possibilities down, we will risk shutting others' dreams down too. Statements such as "that will never work," "you are being too optimistic," "I'll believe it when I see it," "that is way beyond you" and "those are pipe dreams", are all reflective of shutting dreams down. If we believe these statements are justified, it will be in our best interest and the interest of others to reflect on why we are cutting our Self and others off from new possibilities. If we do not believe in possibilities for others, we are not believing in possibilities for our Self.

> Regardless of the injuries we have experienced, it is essential we awaken our desires, dreams, and ideas and follow them for the sake of our Truth. They came to us from the pure essence of Self, and they deserve to be nurtured.

The summer of 1986 preceded our family's move back to the big city. My husband worked at a peach orchard and I found a part-time job at a local café washing dishes to fund this move. Many things were aligning well for us. I could trust the woman next door to care for my babies. Although on a fixed income herself, she would not take more than one third of my minimum wage paycheck for her services. She believed in us and wanted to do her part to support us. We were extremely excited about the next chapter in our lives. This was the summer of big dreams coming to fruition which opened the door to endless possibilities. My husband was accepted to continue his studies at a major university and I had dreams for my future too. Although I was not yet ready to return to school, I knew I would be moving in this direction too. Our move to the city represented opportunity.

The man I worked for at the small café could be quite demeaning. He pretty much interrogated me for the first few weeks asking me endless questions such as: How old were you when you had your first child? Why did you have another one so close? Is your husband the father of both your children? I was just shy of eighteen after the birth of my first child, but I looked fourteen. Clearly I knew this man had a less than optimistic outlook for my life, but my excitement about life outweighed his negativity. He was a rough stepping stone to my dreams and offered me an important life lesson. He showed me that when I am fully engaged in my life, I am less likely to be preoccupied with the negativity of others. I would need to tolerate him only for the summer - which was nothing compared to a whole future.

One day near the end of summer while washing dishes, I was lost in thoughts of new possibilities for my life. At this point I hand washed every dish in that place a thousand times over. Interestingly I had come to experience this repetitive task as meditative. With two young babies at home, both in cloth diapers, I rarely had the opportunity for such solitude. It was the end of the day, the café was quiet, and my boss decided he wanted to chat. Still half into my dreams I freely informed him of this deep desire of mine to go back to school. My mind was shocked back into the land of the living when he responded with a loud grunt; with conviction he told me that this dream would never happen for me.

Perhaps it was because I opened up a deep and sacred desire to someone who did not hold my life with regard, I felt devastated with his shocking response. I stood paralyzed and speechless. The wet dishcloth I held in the clenched fist of my right hand took the brunt of the intense turmoil inside; it vomited water down the front of my apron. I did not care. I had been snapped out of a beautiful dream and into a nightmare. He must have registered my shock as he turned on his heels and left me alone. I retreated into some kind of inner holding tank and counted the minutes before I could leave. I released my tears while waiting for my bus a safe distance away from this man. I was hurt but not destroyed. I had come to see over the months that my boss was not a happy man. He resented his work and blamed events in his life for the feeling he had no other choices. He spoke negatively about many things and many people, not just me. Perhaps I represented a passion he had once known but let go of, and he lashed out on me for this too. Mostly I think I cried over the senseless cruelty of others. Through my tears I seemed to release the pain I had stuffed down; the tears felt surprisingly cathartic.

I came back to work for my final week at the café and found my boss surprisingly pleasant. On my last day he wanted to meet my family; they had come to pick me up. I was surprised by this too. I stood observing with curiosity as he lingered at the van, mesmerized and happy in the presence of my beautiful babies. For the first time I felt I really saw this man underneath his bitterness. I silently wished him peace then I turned my focus towards the future. I forgave him, and this felt incredibly freeing.

Gathering Our Seeds of Wisdom

> *We cannot conceive of matter being formed of nothing, since things require a seed to start from . . . Therefore there is not anything which returns to nothing, but all things return dissolved into their elements.*
> William Shakespeare

Themes of my earlier lessons reemerged over the years, and each time they did I was brought deeper into my Truth. Earlier lessons were the seeds of realization that grew into wisdom. I have come to honor these sparks of Truth. Sometimes I had to work hard in my life to see past dark clouds that shielded my light. Each time I did, there was something familiar I noticed from previous lessons, something deeper than my fear. When I recognized this feeling as clarity I experienced in my Truth, I felt a deep sense of empowerment. I know, as I know the moon rises and exists behind dark clouds, that my Truth is always present; this gives me strength to move through storms because I know I will discover more when I pull my Self in the direction of this light. As reflected in a statement from Buddha, the wisdom of this Truth has been known for thousands of years:

Three things cannot be long hidden: the sun, the moon, and the truth.

Patience is the energy of our Good Wolf; it is a holding tank for frustrations and allows us to come back into our reflective space where we can connect with Self, understand our insecurities more and make better choices for our life. I have come to deeply appreciate the virtue of patience; it helps me get through storms.

The history of the quote "patience is a virtue" cannot accurately be traced. The first known publication of this quote comes from a poem called "Piers Plowman" written over several years between 1360 to 1387 by William Langland in England.[9] The reference to patience is written in Middle English as "suffraunce is a soverayn virtue" which translates to "patience is a sovereign [supreme] virtue." The writer Langland and the character in his dream, Piers Plowman, are on a quest. There are representations of heaven and hell, and in the middle of both is the world of humans, *the field full of folk* which was Langland's main concern. Truth and Salvation, Dowel, Dobet and Dobest [do well, do better and do best], Faith, Hope and Charity are described and explored. The reader is reminded that the choices we make on earth will have eternal consequences. What Langland wrote about is what continues to concern us today. Patience is Good Wolf energy that helps us manage distractions and leads us to the awareness that we do have choices in life. Patience helps us to work towards change as we set our sights further and higher than distractions that demand attention. Developing patience requires practice; the more we practice it, the better we get at it.

---

[9] A number of printed versions of this poem exist; one is: William Langland, *Piers Plowman: A New Annotated Edition of the C-Text*, ed. Derek Pearsall (Exeter: University of Exeter Press, 2008).

We can read many stories and inspirational works informing us of wisdom to help guide us through our worldly difficulties, but words are not enough. It is what we do with words we resonate with that make all the difference in our lives. As the eagle finds its rhythm with wings and wind, we too desire to soar in the natural rhythm of our Selves but we must take our Self out into the world to do this. With each tether we untie we will feel lighter. Our ego and its need to be better, smarter and have more and our fears and insecurities can keep us weighted down like a grounded bird, trapped in a maze surrounded by paradise.

When she was alive, my husband's grandmother told me a beautiful folklore story that spoke to the essence of our human desire to live beyond the clutter that can keep us trapped in our mind:

The Worry Tree[10]

The Carpenter that the farmer hired to help finish restoring an old barn was having a particularly bad day. It was one of those times where everything that could

---

[10] This is a folktale by an unknown author which I have paraphrased.

possibly go wrong did go wrong. All day long the carpenter's equipment for this job broke down. No sooner would he fix a piece of machinery than another would break down. Finally, after a long hard day, the carpenter trudged over to his truck to drive home but his truck would not start. Without hesitation the farmer grabbed his keys and offered to drive this exhausted carpenter home.

Several miles away they pulled into a quaint old farmhouse on a few acres that had been lovingly cared for. The farmer lingered in the driveway and watched the man walk towards an oak tree; when he reached into the tree, it seemed to the farmer as though the carpenter had placed something there. After a short pause at the tree the carpenter walked towards his home but before he reached his front door, the farmer called for him and asked what he was doing at the tree.

The carpenter replied,

"Oh - that is my worry tree. When I come home after a difficult day, I walk over and place my worries in it so I don't bring them home to my family."

The carpenter explained further to the farmer,

"when I leave tomorrow I will pick them up and deal with them, but the funny thing is, most of the worries I place up in the tree are gone when I come to collect them the next day."

How we cope with adversity does influence our ability to be present in positive ways in our lives. What we do to create and preserve space so adversity and other distractions do not consume our lives becomes wisdom which can guide our lives. Bike riding is one activity that helps me to relax and break free of the busyness of my life. It provides me with physical and mental space where I can gain perspective before I enter my own field full of folk again. I have learned many great lessons on my bike rides. For example, I have learned that when I feel exceptionally depleted, I can be quite resistant to leaving the house even though I know a bike ride is exactly what I need to replenish my Self. On these *battle days* (as I have come to see them) I feel like I am dragging the weight of my burdens behind me. The burdens are so firmly attached that I cannot seem to shake them off. I feel like giving in to the weight of them and collapsing into a sedentary state. But I have been down this road enough to know my mind is responding to the messages of burden, and I need to work this out before I can truly relax.

With this awareness I heave forward and drag my Self through the motions of getting ready and onto my bike. With each pedal forward another burden is released. A few miles later, my mind chatter becomes a whisper, and I am more present in the rhythm of my body and the expansive space around me. I no longer feel like I am held captive by my stress. When I am absorbed in the sounds and smells of nature and aware of the gentle greeting of wind sweeping over my face inviting me to breathe it in, I know I have arrived in Self - and I am free.

Like a babe who absorbs the world with no preconscious agenda, we too can create space to be with our Self in the purity of curiosity, being led by our natural propensity towards wonder.

Our jobs, responsibilities, losses and achievements are very important - the experiences we have with them can provide valuable learning which can bring us deeper into our Truth - but they do not need to define us. They are amongst many significant events in our lives that can open us up to our world in profound ways, but we are not meant to be defined by these events. We can run the risk of limiting our Self to other possibilities if we become too attached to one state of being. For example if we feel we do not have time to take care of our Self then we may need to step back and reflect on our priorities. We may need to let go of some other attachments in order for this to happen, but we can make time to nurture our Self. When we think of the kind of Self we want to bring into the lives of our most sacred relationships we will know why it is important to begin with our Self.

Celebrating Our Truth

> *"Pan, who and what art thou?" he [Hook] cried huskily. "I'm youth, I'm joy," Peter answered at a venture, "I'm a little bird that has broken out of the* egg."
> J. M. Barrie, Peter Pan

When I reflect upon the years of observing my daughters grow, I see the most important gift I gave them was to be available to them - so I could help clear a path for their destinies. They showed us their interests, and we helped to find a way for them to explore them. As I got older I would make light of being a young mother who "followed the lead of her kids." There were plenty of opportunities for play because we were a young family who were on a great adventure, and we were doing this together. We are still a family that loves to play together. I had to stop giving airplane rides when my daughter's feet began to scrape the ground but tickling battles continue to this day. What mattered to me greatly was that my children were fair and compassionate to others and that they did not accept something that was not right for them. Doing their best seemed to come naturally for them. They were a part of the rhythm of our lives - not a separate responsibility we had to try and find time for.

We learned that children process information differently from adults - that the messages they hear can influence how they view the world. As my daughters grew into adults, I saw that they had internal resources to work through difficult times. I believe they had a natural awareness from growing up in a family that was open to learning; that it is healthy to learn from mistakes.

This was something I came to see later in my life as I observed my daughters mature into adults. I do not think they struggled as much as I did to locate their Self at an early age. I can see that the most profound gift we can bring into relationships is to navigate through obstacles without losing sight of our Self.

To connect with others from the place of compassion, curiosity, and love we must work through fears, unhealthy ego attachments, and false messages. From this direction life does not become primarily about our needs.

My eldest daughter showed us very early in her life her propensity towards agility. At two she horrified us by fearlessly scrambling up the highest object she could find, laughing at our efforts to reach her. At three she taught herself to ride a bike, and soon after she was whizzing around on roller blades and ice skates. By five she wanted to play lacrosse, and we found her a team. There were no girls' lacrosse teams at that time in our district so she played with the boys. Soon she was playing in a competitive division. This beautiful girl with long, dark, thick curly hair discarded her dresses for track suits, sports shorts and running shoes. She was in high demand for neighborhood street hockey and basketball, and just like her boy pals, threw off her shirt when too encumbered by it. I did not think twice about this; no one did. It just seemed natural for her.

One day while camping I was sitting a distance away on the grass watching her play on the park zip line. I was engrossed in her spirit. The wild long hair in her ponytail moved with the same abandon as she did. Her lean ten-year-old body glistened in the sun. She wore sports shorts and nothing else. She was in her bliss. A man was sitting not too far from me and greeted his son who returned from the playground. My attention shifted to the conversation beside me as it became apparent both father and son were captivated by my daughter.

"Dad" asked the son,

"Is that kid a boy or a girl?"

I shifted my glance back to the wild child flying in the air. The father intently contemplated the situation and answered his son:

"I think he is a little Indian boy."

I smiled inside and just let it be. But as I sat their watching her, I recognized she was coming to an age when she would need to put her shirt on. This deeply saddened me.

The following summer began much the same. Her shirt came off. I told her,

"Honey, you need to keep your shirt on; you're eleven years-old now. Soon your body will change; if you don't wear a shirt this will become a big problem for you."

Predictably, she protested,

"I don't care if anyone has a problem with it."

Although it pained me tremendously, I persisted,

"This is not an option; you need to keep your shirt on when you're outside of the house."

I saw her handle herself with others, and I knew her Self-esteem was strong. I was not worried about this. I was proud of her inner strength and zest for life. I was worried about the dangers she did not perceive; this is a loss of innocence that I grieved.

I knew she was taking her shirt off when she was out of my sight because her friend's mother informed me when my daughter arrived at their house to play hockey, shirtless. I allowed my daughter these moments as I knew she needed time to transition and grieve this loss herself. Many of the parents were sad too, but we all understood why girls needed to dress differently. We were reminded of a time in our lives where we too grieved the passing of innocence. No wonder my daughter adores Peter Pan!

This daughter of mine is now thirty and a mother of a beautiful two-year-old boy, my first grandchild. The importance of play and adventure is strongly reflected in her relationship with her son. She has never let go of her zest for life; I see her bring this spirit into everything she does. Her love for the outdoors and her desire to engage in adventure has not changed. In her career as a teacher she has found purpose in working in alternative schools where kids have not managed in the mainstream system for various reasons. It seems the more profound the adversity these kids face, the stronger my daughter's curiosity becomes about the child underneath the fear. The joy she feels when they have discovered something about themselves reveals Peter Pan magic she has never let go.

I remember vividly her enthusiasm as she told me about the boy who was sent to the alternate school because he could not focus on books. She said he was assessed as being too disruptive for the mainstream classroom. My daughter observed his interest in rap music and rejoiced when this boy, whom she knew was bright, excelled in his lessons when they were to write and record a rap song about history. I was told he sang about his history and that his performance was compelling. From being a boy whom no one could handle to suddenly becoming a boy people were compelled to hear affirmed this boy's experience and gave him room to explore and play with his gifts. He was seen, and he thrived.

Creating an environment where children are encouraged to explore and learn through discovery of Self, is a reflection of my little Peter Pan who refused to allow herself to step completely out of Never Neverland.

Embracing our Light of Truth

> *Truth will ultimately prevail where there is pains to bring it to light.*
> George Washington

As our seeds of Truth become realized, we will see our Self. As we continue to nurture our desires, interests and appreciation of the wonders around us we will want to open our life up more to these experiences.

From the place of our Truth we will come to know that if someone is intentionally trying to undermine our happiness; it may be hurtful to experience this, but the insecurity is not ours. If we internalize these projections and take them personally it does become our insecurity to work through. Not everyone will be happy for us. But we can be happy for our Self and share this joy with people who do celebrate each other. These are our kindred souls, and they put a spring in our step. If we appease others' envy by lowering our Self, if we internalize criticism that is not constructive, stay in environments that are not healthy for us, project frustrations or try to control others, we will feed our Bad Wolf and interrupt our true destiny. People who have been through immense adversity and come out on the other side of it generally do not take the beauty in this life for granted. They humble me, and they are my greatest teachers.

The challenges we face can bring us deeper into our Selves because we must venture deeper to rise above them. What we learn will make all the difference in how we navigate future adversity.

Not very long ago in a quiet and reflective moment in my bedroom I observed a significant event. It was in the evening at the beginning of summer. I had come up to my bedroom to fold laundry and instead I laid on my bed and drifted into the beautiful colors of the sunset and the songs of gathering birds singing the joy of another day well spent. I observed a fly buzzing around my room, slowly and methodically, taking resting breaks between intervals of searching for a route back outside. I made a mental note to open the window without a screen so the fly could find its way back outside. Unlike some flies who buzz around when trapped, thrashing themselves against a window until they collapse and die from exhaustion, this fly did not elicit any sense of urgency. Unfortunately my mind shifted away from being present in the moment and back into focusing on the task I had come up to do. I forgot about the fly.

It was not until the next morning, when I heard the same calm buzzing, that I remembered the fly. She had rested all night and was now focused on the window without a screen where she had most likely entered the day before. The fly was slowly and methodically walking around the edge of the window assessing the situation. Empathizing with her plight, I gently opened the window and she flew out in such a way that I would have never known she had spent the past twenty-four hours trapped in a foreign world. I thanked the fly for this lesson in patience, perseverance and never giving up on hope.

Events in our life can challenge us in unimaginable ways, but they cannot take the essence of who we are away unless we let them. Our determination to come back to Self and rise with Self requires us to pull harder and go deeper than we have had to go before. What we discover along the way will awaken many Truths that we will nurture for the rest of our life. In this way we come to look back on our adversities as profound awakenings to our Self. What we may have once been terrified of, we no longer fear as much - we now have wisdom to help us through future adversity.

To have our hearts accessible once again to the pleasure of laughter, the beautiful cycle of seasons, a random smile, frolics in nature, gratitude for life, time with loved ones; these are the moments we rediscover our True Selves in more profound and everlasting ways. It is this awareness that stops us from turning away from our Truth and motivates us to deal with weeds.

CHAPTER FOUR

BEING IN OUR WORLD WITH TRUTH

It is not the language of painters but the language of nature which one should listen to, the feeling for the things themselves, for reality is more important than the feeling for pictures.
Vincent Van Gogh

The process of working through layers of pain, insecurities, ego defenses and false messages is not a race; we are simply becoming aware of blocks that have prevented us from living in the world with our Truth. With each layer we work through, another Truth is revealed and we move into a deeper and more authentic connection to our world.

We can become sensitive to the injuries we have suffered in this world and risk hiding away out of fear that we will be harmed again. We can also feel entitled in this world when we have learned to believe that we are more special and deserving than others. The energy we invest in defending these positions, whether it is isolating in our homes or behind a False Self, keeps us preoccupied with our individual insecurities and/or needs.

When we nurture Truth we see the state of our world more clearly because we are not disconnected from it. With this awareness our desire to be present in our world in positive ways becomes more significant than any injuries our ego may have suffered.

If we resist seeing what is real and uncomfortable, we are not opening doors to our life.

Nurturing Healthy Relationships

> *If civilization is to survive, we must cultivate the science*
> *of human relationships - the ability of all peoples, of all*
> *kinds, to live together, in the same world at peace.*
> Franklin D. Roosevelt

When we are motivated to nurture our Self with love and kindness we will also relate to others in this way and create opportunities for growth. There will be times we will choose to sacrifice time for our Self to give to others because of our natural propensity towards love. Whether they be our children, partners, friends and neighbors there will be times we will give more to others than to our Self as we assist and support them at times of need. Likewise we may need to rely on others for extra support to help us through difficult times. There may be times of immense turmoil that require a great deal of energy and drive we may not have previously realized we had. Rebuilding lives after a natural disaster is a good example of times where humanity calls upon great strength and love to survive and/or to assist others through difficult times.

From the direction of our Truth, the energy we give to help

others enables them to help themselves. This feels good and worth the energy we give. When we have given what we can, we will need to turn our attention back to our Self and replenish our internal resources through Self-care. Giving is beautiful and natural and includes giving back to our Self; it is when we are giving in unhealthy ways that we feel depleted, used and negative about giving.

Imbalance can indicate that we need to explore new possibilities and awaken previously discovered wisdom that we may have abandoned. No matter what we discover, the journey of *bringing our Self back to balance* is a profound reminder that at any point in time we can all sway too far from our True Self path. There are no shortcuts to working through our fears and learning new wisdom - no one can do this for us. It certainly is healthy to seek support and tools to help us along the way, but no one can walk our path for us. If we become too dependent on others to do this, we will burden them with our responsibilities and insecurities and will deplete others of resources they need to live a balanced life. Our Truth lies beneath our fears, and it leads us to freedom.

> What we nurture in our Self is what we will bring into our relationships. If we nurture love and regard for our Self, we will desire the same for others.

A few years back when dear friends of ours were getting married, I was reflecting on thoughts of being in a relationship with love. An image of *unity* came to my mind, and I felt it to be beautiful; I knew these were the thoughts I would share with our friends on their wedding day. Later I felt inspired to share the same words with my niece and her husband on their wedding day. The unity image came from a place of love, and I find it helps guide me in all my relationships:

Two souls flowing through life converge; each reaches for the other and they clasp their hands in a profound connection of unity. The other hand is left free to explore and to connect to the large, infinite space of our physical and spiritual worlds.

One hand is holding on to the soul mate, feeling the connection of love and commitment to working towards balance and unity of a shared space. The clasped hands are a reminder to the soul of what we feel when we converge and why we remain connected.

The free hand is symbolic of our need to tend to our Self needs: our interests, work, spirituality, our physical health and our significant connections to others.

No matter where we go, we bring our Self along. Our relationships with others, both negative and positive, can teach us a great deal about our Self. For one, if we ignore our Self in a relationship, we will suffer; if we ignore the other in a relationship, they will suffer. Like Bad and Good Wolves, whatever we nurture will grow.

Everyone deserves to be treated with the same regard we wish for our Self. Where we are born and whom we are born to influences the resources we have access to, but it does not make us more or less deserving than others. If we treat others with the expectation that they should give to us because we perceive they have resources we are lacking, we will not be treating them with loving regard. If we treat others as less than us because they do not have the resources we possess, we will not be treating them with loving regard. When we desire to help our brothers and sisters access opportunities that enhance their survival, we will be motivated from love. If we are motivated for any other reason other than love, we may need to reflect on which wolf we are feeding. We discover that when we have mutual love and regard for each other, our differences and disagreements become lessons of listening, communicating, patience, and resolution.

Tommy Douglas (October 20, 1904 - February 24, 1986) is a man I have come to respect in Canadian history. His life work, to improve the lives of all Canadians, continues to benefit Canada today. He was a Scottish-born Canadian Baptist minister before becoming the social democratic politician who began a grassroots movement in Saskatchewan in the 1940s. He and his party members advocated for accessible universal social support programs for all citizens of Canada, not just the elite. Tommy's work was paramount in the development of the universal health care system in Canada which continues to benefit Canadians today. His deep passion and drive for improving the lives of those less fortunate has made him a legendary role model, a great Canadian. Here is a wonderful quote from Tommy Douglas's speech on the Humanity First Policy:[11]

We believe that every man is his brother's keeper. We believe that those that are strong ought to help bear the burdens of the weak. We believe that any society is

---

[11] Tommy Douglas, "Humanity First" (Policy Speech, 1944).

measured by what is does for the aged, the sick, the orphans and the less fortunate that live in our midst.

I believe that love is stronger than hate, that the outstretched hand is more powerful than the clenched fist, that in the long run feeding the hungry and clothing the naked and lifting up the fallen will do more to establish peace in the world than all the bombs and guns we can make.

This is the policy of humanity first . . .

To have another believe in our dreams and cheer for us as we explore them is a true blessing that should never be taken for granted. This support and encouragement is a gift to be treasured and reciprocated so that the other can also experience the power of such unconditional love. If our relationships are one-sided - if one always gives and the other receives - the relationship is not in balance. Likewise, if we stay in a Self-depriving relationship because we fear change, we will find our Self feeling depleted. As we turn back towards our deprived Self and work towards balance in our life, we may find there are some connections we will need to let go of because our attachments to them pull us back to a place where we can no longer be. We will discover a great deal about our Self on our way back to our own path.

> The further we walk forward along our path, the more absorbed we will become in the vast open space surrounding our life. We will feel free, empowered, and lighter.

Being Inspired by Others

> *You are not here merely to make a living. You are here in order to enable the world to live more amply, with greater vision, with a finer spirit of hope and achievement. You are here to enrich the world, and you impoverish yourself if you forget the errand.*
> Woodrow Wilson

Some of the most remarkable people throughout history are those who were driven by compassion and desire, working toward creating opportunities for the betterment of others and fairness for all. There are also those people who are infamously remembered as being driven by individual agendas, anger and revenge. We have the capability to be either. We choose which wolf to feed. To direct our energy toward love and fairness is truly a testament to the eternal power of our Good Wolf and opens us up to our world.

If we focus too much on our individual needs, we will develop disconnection from our Self and others. If we believe it is our right to be given things from others or that others should be deprived for our gain, we will feed the Bad Wolf. Jealousy, resentment, and entitlement - as well as bitterness, anger, and hate - are born from such ill-conceived beliefs.

> When we keep our focus on being available to others with a loving Self - this will make all the difference.

It is the selfless acts of kindness from others that feed our soul; yet if our heart is not open we will close the door to these gifts. If we can imagine what it feels like to give a gift from our heart only to have it scrutinized, mishandled, and then tossed aside, we can understand how experiences such as this can create a feeling of distrust of others - yet we need to be in our world with our authentic Self. If we feel proud of our power over others and identify through tactics of intimidation and disregard for others, we are nurturing an insecure False Self which can only be maintained by causing others harm. A well nurtured True Self does not accept such treatment - instead energy is redirected towards connecting to others in their Truth, not their False Self. To those beautiful, kindhearted people that have retreated inward because of pain caused by others, I have a message for you:

> Please know your love is far more beautiful, needed, and everlasting than the pain you have retreated from. Please come out and explore the world from the place of your true beauty; come discover the wonders that speak to your soul and nurture these, for this is where your Truth will be realized. The world needs your love.

When we understand that being treated with kindness is not our right, we will open our hearts to our Self and to others and will be less likely to take loving acts of kindness from others for granted. Many of these lessons I learned from my children. Their pure love and trust in me woke me up to my Self in profound ways. If I was too selfish or too insecure I would deny them what they needed from me. This awareness brought me deeper into my Truth. I remember one such lesson when my daughters were young while on a bike riding trip.

My joy of bike riding began in my early childhood. The discovery that my body could operate an object that brought so much freedom and wonder to my life continues to feel beyond amazing. As years went by, I graduated from riding in the parameters of my neighborhood block to visiting friend's miles away. I took detours through fields and forests, whizzed down hills as fast as I could go and charged through mud puddles with my legs straddled high in the air; the bigger the puddle, the bigger the splash. I had crashes for sure, but they were just a price I paid for joy.

There were several years, when my daughters were very young, that I took a hiatus from riding. As soon as they could coordinate all parts of their body, I introduced them to the mechanical wonder on wheels. They learned to ride two-wheelers early, and soon they too were experiencing the endless wonders of the bicycle. To be back on my own bike again was like reuniting with a dear old friend. I was more responsible when I rode with my children, but it did not take me long to reawaken my desire for the old thrills of air, wind and speed. For the most part I satisfied these urges on solo rides through endless trails that surrounded our lush, west coast neighborhood.

As my daughters grew, I expanded our riding territory and took them on adventures to local campgrounds and beyond.

Some of the trails we discovered were so amazing that the temptation to be a little more reckless felt too great for me to dismiss. In this case, I would inform my daughters I had to ride forward to check if the trail was safe enough to proceed. They knew the routine; I would go ahead and then holler for them to come if the trail was safe. As soon as I was out of their view I would take off like the proverbial bat out of hell, churning up dirt, rebounding off protruding tree roots and other objects; then I would come back to stillness on earth, at which point I would call for them. I felt both exhilarated and naughty.

This deception all changed the summer my girls were eight and ten years old. We were on a five-day camping trip, just the three of us. We were not in familiar territory, and I was conscious of keeping them close by. We rode our bikes all day, every day and discovered many new trails. On our last day we found the most amazing, gently sloping, winding trail through a beautiful western red cedar forest. The trees were huge, and so were their rounded roots, rising up from the path. We paused on a knoll with breathtaking beauty and allowed our senses to absorb the wonder around us. The sun was streaming through the forest in dancing rays, giving the impression the light was alive and being orchestrated by magical forest fairies. The aroma of sundrenched cedar was thick, permeating, and invigorating. To the left just down from the knoll was a pond glistening like diamonds through the trees. The forest was loud and animated with birds of various species. They flew back and forth across the pond with reckless abandon, careless of others in their path. They smashed into the water then quickly rose as they were eager to get to the other side so they could repeat this water-smashing thrill.

I lost focus on my responsibilities. I allowed my mind to become entranced by the forest energy and turned my focus to the thrill ride that might lay ahead of me. I entertained rationalizing thoughts – "It will be quick. The girls have a safe place to wait. How could I refuse such an opportunity?" In a matter of seconds I allowed my False Self to be completely convinced by my Bad Wolf that it would be okay to toss my Good Wolf aside.

"Mommy is going to go ahead and make sure the trail is safe; I'll call you when I see it is okay for you to come."

They knew the drill, and they complied without question. They believed I was looking out for their safety, not deceiving them for my own selfish interest.

The excitement was too much. My body, guided by my unleashed mind was shaking with the reckless abandon of a forest creature. As soon as I was out of sight of my precious daughters I sped forward, leaving those two innocent trusting souls behind in the cloud of earth I dug up and spat out behind me. Root after wonderful root I hit and laughed in manic joy as I was sent rebounding into the air.

I was definitely more reckless than usual.

Just ahead of me, at the bottom of the long meandering hill, was a large protruding root; I decided that striking this was going to be the grand finale before I called for the girls to come. Full of false confidence, I rushed towards the root but did not anticipate a slight turn of the path. Immediately after making contact with the root I knew this particular risk was not going to turn out well. My bike flew high into the air, tossing me off. I came down on top of the root with a thud and my bike followed, landing directly on top of me. Draped over the root, my bike and I were a twisted ball of metal and human, lying helpless on the forest floor.

For a few seconds I could not move. I thought of my beautiful daughters; I would need to call them to help me, and I felt immense shame. I listened for sounds of others to help me and save my daughters (and myself) from facing the repercussions of my shame, but I heard nothing. My body was intact, and I began to feel it again. Everything worked, but I was still immobilized with the shock of the fall. I had the wind - or should I say the ego - knocked right out of me. I was pinned to the earth underneath my bike.

The girls would now be wondering about me. I needed help. I had to call for them. In the calmest voice I could muster I sent the message back up the path I had descended.

"Okay girls, you can come now."

My announcement was met with an excited and trusting,

"Okay mommy, we're coming."

I could do nothing but wait.

Being free of my ego, my world came into focus. It was no more than a few minutes before my girls reached me, but my thoughts were vivid and lasting. With my head planted firmly on the ground I focused on a tiny black ant whose attentiveness to life gave no room for concerning himself with me. My last thought before my daughters whizzed around the corner was to the ant - "I feel so much smaller than you, my friend."

Quickly as I heard them coming around the last corner before reaching me, I plastered a smile on my face. When they came into view, I called out in the most playful voice I could muster,

"Hi girls, mommy slipped."

For a split second they looked confused and took a few seconds to reorganize their thoughts from excitement to shock. I had anticipated this response and downplayed the whole ordeal.

"Hey, don't worry! I'm fine. I'm just a little stuck. Could you please lift the bike off mommy?"

The looks of immense worry as they struggled to lift my bike off shifted to expressions of relief when they saw I could move. I kept a permanent smile on my face for their benefit, but I felt shame. If their mother was lying helpless on the forest floor entangled with her bike, this certainly did not look like a safe trail to them. We sat for a few minutes before proceeding forward. I needed to say more. They needed to be validated.

"I was going too fast; I was irresponsible, and I was not being safe. It's not the forest's fault I hurt myself; it is my fault."

"Mommy, you really scared us," my eldest daughter stated.

"Yeah, mommy, we thought you were really badly hurt," chimed in my youngest daughter.

I received a lengthy lecture on being irresponsible and agreed without question or correction. Only when they hopped back on their bikes did I feel it was okay to get back onto mine. I knew I had some trust to build.

When I think of my beautiful daughters forgiving me for being dishonest with them and causing them distress because of a selfish action on my part, it becomes easier for me to forgive others in this same way. I have learned that if we are to deepen our experience here on earth in everlasting and loving ways, we will need to make a regular practice of taming our ego (come back to our Self on earth), recognize and work through our fear and pain (lift our Self back up to our place on earth), and forgive our Self and others along the way (clear our path of clutter).

Although at times they were quite difficult, I am thankful for my lessons. They taught me the power of forgiveness and courage and brought me deeper into my Truth.

Discovering Truth in a Structured World

When you were born, you cried
and the world rejoiced.
Live your life
so that when you die,
the world cries and you rejoice.
Native American Proverb

Our human world is very much structured around economics; this value can lead us down a path of individualistic needs in which each of us strives to have more. If we identify our worth based upon material wealth, we will run the risk of becoming too disconnected from the natural world and our True Selves.

Throughout history we see the best and the worst of people during times of turmoil. During great natural disasters, people who have lost their material wealth will come together and assist others regardless of class, religion or race because what matters the most is life, not possessions. The greatest stains in our history mark times when we disregarded lives for selfish gains of wealth and power and retaliated with hate.

When, in the face of great adversity, we rise with forgiveness and a desire to love, we work towards change that will be for the benefit of all, not just a few. In this direction we learn from historical mistakes and stop cycles of hate - we learn about the cost of revenge and do not desire to perpetuate it. When this Truth is seen in the face of atrocity, it shines brighter and more eternally than the darkness it penetrated. Love and forgiveness cannot be ignored. I cannot think of a more powerful quote speaking to this Truth than these words spoken by the former president of South Africa - Nelson Mandela:

> No one is born hating another person because of the color of his skin, or his background, or his religion. People must learn to hate, and if they can learn to hate, they can be taught to love, for love comes more naturally to the

human heart than it's opposite.[12]

A powerful event of love rising above hate occurred along the Western Front during World War I and is known as The Christmas Truce.

On December 7, 1914 Pope Benedict XV suggested a temporary hiatus of the war to celebrate Christmas. Germany agreed, but the other powers refused[13]

The Pope had planted a seed, and it germinated in the minds of the German troops on one side and British troops on the other. After a night of singing Christmas carols to each other from their respective trenches, the Germans emerged on Christmas morning unarmed and shook hands with their enemy soldiers. British and German soldiers wished each other a Merry Christmas in the other's native tongue. Cigarettes were exchanged, pictures were taken, soccer games were played and carols were sung. There have been

---

[12] Nelson Mandela, *Long Walk to Freedom* [(New York: Hachette Book Group, 2013)], [p. 622].

[13] Terry Philpot, "World War I's Pope Benedict XV and the pursuit of peace," *National Catholic Reporter*, July 19, 2014, accessed June 1, 2015, http://ncronline.org/news/peace-justice/world-war-pope-benedict-xv-and-pursuit-peace.

Hollywood films[14] based on this event and books written
about it.[15]

A letter Captain A.D. Chater of the 2nd Battalion Gordon
Highlanders, sent to his mother over one hundred years ago[16],
is reflective of the light of love penetrating darkness.

> I think I have seen today one of the most extraordinary
> sights that anyone has ever seen. About 10 o'clock this
> morning I was peeping over the parapet when I saw a
> German, waving his arms, and presently two of them
> got out of their trenches and came towards ours.
>
> We were just going to fire on them when we saw they
> had no rifles. So one of our men went to meet them and
> in about two minutes the ground between the two lines
> of trenches was swarming with men and officers of both
> sides, shaking hands and wishing each other a happy
> Christmas.

---

[14]*Joyeux Noel,* directed by Christian Carion (New York: Sony Pictures
Classics, 2005)
[15] Stanley Weintraub and K. Harris, *Silent Night: The Story of the World
War I Christmas Truce* (Toronto: The Free Press, 2001).
[16] "Letters from the front - the Christmas truce," Royal Mail Group,
accessed April 28, 2015, http://www.royalmailgroup.com/about-
us/heritage/letters-front-%E2%80%93-christmas-truce.

Captain Chater later wrote to his mother:

> We had another parlay with the Germans in the middle.
> We exchanged cigarettes and autographs, and some
> more people took photos. I don't know how long it will
> go on for - I believe it was supposed to stop yesterday,
> but we can hear no firing going on along the front today
> except a little distant shelling. We are, at any rate,
> having another truce on New Year's Day, as the
> Germans want to see how the photos come out!

Opening Our Self Up to Difficult Truths

> *The earth is supported by the power of truth; it is the*
> *power of truth that makes the sun shine and the winds*
> *blow; indeed all things rest upon truth.*
> Chanakya

I have been thinking more about how I participate in the field
full of folk . . . how we all, to some degree or another,
participate in the driving of our economy. I was at a party
recently and was sitting across from a man who works in the
oil sands of Alberta, Canada. He was asked by another guest
in a friendly manner about his work, and he responded in a

defensive way which made me think he had been previously challenged for what he does.

"Everyone uses oil who drives a car; we are not the only bad guys," he responded.

I agreed wholeheartedly and so did the others around our table. As difficult as this can be to face, I know that I, along with most people existing on earth, do contribute to the destruction on our planet. We are all responsible and accountable for this. Our economy is driven by what we perceive as our needs.

> We can point fingers and blame others, but we cannot avoid that change exists within each and every one of us.

I was again reminded of this truth recently when my youngest daughter brought to my attention the planned culling of one hundred and eighty-four wolves over the next four years in the South Selkirk region of British Columbia, Canada; this area shares a border with Washington State and Idaho, USA. Wolves are going to be culled because endangered caribou herds are an important source of food for the wolves. The caribou herd is estimated to have dwindled from forty-six in

2009 to eighteen at last count (in March of 2014). There are other such culls of wildlife throughout North America for similar reasons. Killing wolves by sharpshooters in helicopters is seen as a humane and quick way to deal with this problem. However the bigger problem is habitat loss, not wolves.

Habitat is easy to take, but much more difficult to recover. This is something all humanity is responsible for. In many instances, such as the South Selkirk region, there is actually enough land to sustain caribou, but changes to the landscape related to forestry, roads, and other forms of development and recreation such as snowmobiling have fragmented the habitat, making it easier for wolves to hunt. The long-term focus in British Columbia is to restore habitat and set restrictions on development and recreation such as snowmobiling, but it can take decades before these measures can have a significant and positive impact in bringing habitat back into balance.[17]

The wolf story made me think of the ways I live on earth. I participate in destructive practices on earth. I drive a car, I buy

---

[17] "Recovery Strategy for the Woodland Caribou, Southern Mountain population (*Rangifer tarandus caribou*) in Canada," Government of Canada, Species at Risk Act Public Registry, last modified February 19, 2015, accessed March 10, 2015, http://www.registrelep-sararegistry.gc.ca/document/default_e.cfm?documentID=1309.

products with packaging, I am not always aware of the ethical practices of the production of my food or other products I buy. I can see that by opening my Self up to the truth of these destructive ways of living, I am becoming increasingly conscious of the consumer choices I make. I feel immense gratitude for those around our beautiful world who work endlessly in raising awareness of our destructive practices on earth and advocate for change, I thank you from the bottom of my heart for your efforts. You do make a difference.

With 7.3 billion people and counting living on earth, just by existing we humans have a tremendous impact on our beautiful planet. When we consider *how* we live on earth, our impact to this planet is even more devastating. There is not one place on earth the practices of our living does not negatively affect, yet we can reduce our impact by making changes in the way we live. As difficult as it to face unpleasant truths, we must help our Self do this to motivate change.

I cannot believe how much I personally need to change concerning the way I live on this planet. Every time I awaken to one Truth another is revealed. I am learning. Currently I am finding excessive plastic packaging weighs heavily on my conscience. The making of plastic requires non-renewable resources that, when transformed, become persistent pollutants that are extremely destructive to our planet. As consumers we drive this destruction because marketers have found that we are attracted to products that are presented in elaborate packaging designed to illicit a pleasure response that entices us to purchase.[18] Then we rip the package apart in a matter of seconds to access our object of desire, discarding the package that no longer has a purpose.

In a similar fashion we use and dispose of countless plastic bottles designed to conveniently provide instant gratification for our thirst. I am blessed to live in a part of the world that has safe drinking water that can easily be placed in a reusable drinking utensil. Even so, whole aisles full of plastic bottles gathered in batches and wrapped in more plastic are prominently featured in food and convenience stores. We chug earth's precious liquids down in a matter of minutes then toss the toxic capsule back to earth as our thank you. We who consume such bottled drinks drive the market for them.

Plastic and other waste is discarded several ways. Much of it

---

[18] T.W. Whitfield and T.J. Wiltshire, "Color psychology: a critical review," *Genet Soc Gen Psychol Monogr.* Vol 116#4 (November 1990), 385-411, accessed March 10, 2015, http://www.ncbi.nlm.nih.gov/pubmed/2289687.

is recycled; much of it goes into massive landfills where our precious earth is ripped apart, habitat displaced and garbage buried deep within earth's soil. Life-giving nutrients are replaced by toxic waste rendering the landfill uninhabitable.[19] The more garbage we humans dispose of, the more land we need. Much of our garbage ends up in earth's oceans.

Five major gyres (regions where currents push water and floating debris in an inward circular motion) occur in our world's oceans. Two of these gyres are the home of the Great Pacific Garbage Patch and the North Atlantic Garbage Patch. Each year we humans globally produce about 280 million tons of plastic,[20] and about 10 percent of this waste ends up in the ocean.[21]

Depending on where we live, our garbage will find its way to one of these gyres. In the Central and North Pacific Ocean our

---

[19] H. Koren and M.S. Bisesi, *Handbook of Environmental Health* (Boca Raton: Lewis Publishers, 2003).

[20] "First estimates suggest around 4% increase in plastics global production from 2010," Plastics Europe, accessed March 19, 2015, http://www.plasticseurope.org/information-centre/press-releases/press-releases-2012/first-estimates-suggest-around-4-increase-in-plastics-global-production-from-2010.aspx.

[21] M. Eriksen et al, "Plastic Pollution in the World's Oceans: More than 5 Trillion Plastic Pieces Weighing over 250,000 Tons Afloat at Sea." *PLoS ONE,* December 20, 2014, accessed March 10, 2015, http://journals.plos.org/plosone/article?id=10.1371/journal.pone.0111913.

waste moves into the Great Pacific Garbage Patch which is estimated to be the size of Texas; it is a wasteland of floating plastic and chemical sludge which varies in density. The North Atlantic Garbage Patch is estimated to extend from Virginia to Cuba. Much of the waste is not seen by the human eye or even from satellites because the plastic has broken down into very small pieces, often lying beneath the ocean's surface.

The small island of Midway Atoll sits in the middle of the Great Pacific Garbage Patch, 1,200 miles from civilization; these islands are home to 1.5 million Layson Albatross. Midway receives twenty tons of plastic debris annually on its shores, and all the albatross are affected by this. One third of albatross chicks die because they are being fed plastic by their parents. When the adults are found dead, their digestive systems are full of plastic.[22] It was extremely difficult for me to not stop myself from researching this further. The graphic images I saw in a documentary titled *Plastic Paradise: The Great Pacific Garbage Patch*[23] left no room to doubt that what

---

[22] John Klavitter, "Discarded Plastics Distress Albatross Chicks," US Fish and Wildlife Service, Open Spaces, October 24, 2012, accessed March 10, 2015, http://www.fws.gov/news/blog/index.cfm/2012/10/24/Discarded-plastics-distress-albatross-chicks.

[23] Angela Sun, *Plastic Paradise: The Great Pacific Garbage Patch,* independent film, 2013, accessed April 28, 2015, http://plasticparadisemovie.com/.

I read was true.

The Layson Albatross is just one of many oceanic life forms impacted by this horrible mess humanity has created. We cannot clean these small particles of plastic up. If we try to siphon this toxin out of the ocean, we will cause more harm by filtering out small, fragile ocean life. We can only stop contributing to this waste and allow nature to break our garbage down over hundreds of years.

Our awareness does influence our choices and does drive change in the consumer market.

What if most people on earth responded by changing the way we live our life . . . by making a conscious effort to not purchase disposable products? What if instead of being attracted to excessive packaging we were repulsed in the awareness of such senseless and destructive waste to our planet? Each of us can make our own choices about what we need. We can organize our lives to filter our water and use a reusable water bottle for convenience when we leave home.

We are capable of change. In the late nineteen seventies researchers proved to us the massive ozone hole above the

Antarctic was being caused by products we were using. This awareness led to the establishment of the Montreal Protocol on Substances that Deplete the Ozone Layer which was put into force in 1989; it is an international treaty that was created to protect the ozone layer. The objective of this treaty is to phase out the production of substances that are responsible for ozone depletion. Certain products we were using containing CFCs (chlorofluorocarbon - the organic compound in aerosols - and other products that contain carbon, chlorine and fluorine) were rapidly thinning our ozone. A recent study[24] showed that if it were not for the Montreal Protocol the ozone hole would have become 40% bigger by 2013. The Montreal Protocol shows us that we can make a positive difference to our world when we change, but we must do this together. We do not have to wait for government-imposed legislation to happen before we change the way we live. We consumers drive the markets. Our awareness is already driving important change. For example, more of us want biodegradable, nontoxic cleaning products because we are aware our cleaning products reenter water sources where other life lives. We are no longer as a whole disbelieving that our abuse of the planet

[24] M. P. Chipperfield, S. S. Dhomse, W. Feng, R. L. McKenzie, G.J.M. Velders & J. A. Pyle, "Quantifying the ozone and ultraviolet benefits already achieved by the Montreal Protocol," *Nature Communications* 6, Article number 7233 (2015), | doi: 10.1038/ncomms8233.

is contributing to climate change. I wonder how our better choices will make a difference to our planet over time. I wonder.

Awakening to the Truth of Our Natural World

We did not think of the great open plains, the beautiful rolling hills, the winding streams with tangled growth, as "wild". Only to the white man was nature a "wilderness" and only to him was it "infested" with "wild" animals and "savage" people. To us it was tame. Earth was bountiful and we were surrounded with the blessings of the Great Mystery[25].

Chief [Luther] Standing Bear

Recently I headed out of the field full of folk with my husband for a weekend in nature. We stopped at a grocery store for supplies, and I found myself walking down an aisle of drinks in plastic bottles. No longer able to tune out the truth of these toxic cylinders, I walked slowly, taking time to look at the massive abundance of plastic. All I could think about was the North Pacific Gyre and the Layson Albatross. Other images

---

[25] Luther Standing Bear, *Land of the Spotted Eagle, New Edition.* (Lincoln: University of Nebraska Press, 2014) Kobo e-book, Chapter 2.

came to my mind: beautiful sea life entangled in our garbage, whales trapped in fishing nets, seagulls entangled in plastic six-pack rings. Some time ago I became conscious of the need to cut the plastic rings so I could help prevent this horrible suffering. On some level, I knew there was a possibility of this plastic reaching wildlife outside of the field full of folk.

I must have been in that aisle for about fifteen minutes. Later my husband told me he saw me in a trance-like state, slowly walking down the aisle of plastic bottles and finally emerging empty-handed. In much of the world, we have the ability to filter water and reduce this unnecessary waste, yet there is such a demand for water in plastic. We have a great deal of *unlearning* to do.

> In the process of awakening to a deeper relationship with this beautiful world of ours, I feel a deeper awakening within my Self.

When we ignore our uncomfortable responses to our history, the plight of our fellow humans and the state of our planet, we can cut our Self off from awareness that touches the essence of Truth that we need to see. When we follow our awakenings, we broaden our awareness and do become motivated towards positive change.

The practice of mindfulness is a constant reminder to be guided by compassion and love for our Self and for others. It is the journey of moving out of our individualistic, False Self and into the interconnected Truth of our Self in relationship with our world. If we stop our Self from contemplating this connection, we will cut our Self off from seeing the harm we can cause and our potential to work towards change.

> No matter how we rationalize our unhealthy behaviors, or find others who agree with them, it is never OK to cause harm.

Unless we consciously bring our Self outside of the structure we live within, we will risk accepting the resources for living that are presented to us without question. Authentic living is being on a constant journey of internal growth through interconnectedness; this includes the environment we live in. When we leave the confinement of the cities we live in and pull our Self away from the structured routines of our lives we learn not to fear the natural world in which we were born to be part of. We have a greater difficulty causing harm to what we are connected to and love.

Black Elk (December 1, 1863 - August 19 1950) was an extraordinary Lakota Sioux teacher and healer. He had many visions in his life which encompassed great wisdom and gave his people much needed strength. The famous "Black Elk's Vision" is taken from his account of a vision he experienced when he was nine years old, very ill and unresponsive for several days. I cannot think of a better statement to close this chapter:

> I was standing on the highest mountain of them all, and round about beneath me was the whole hoop of the world. And while I stood there I saw more than I can tell and I understood more than I saw; for I was seeing in a sacred manner the shapes of all things in the spirit, and the shape of all shapes as they must live together like one being. And I saw the sacred hoop of my people was one of many hoops that made one circle, wide as daylight as starlight, and in the center grew one mighty flowering tree to shelter all children of one mother and one father. And I saw that it was holy.[26]

---

[26] Black Elk and John G. Neihardt, *Black Elk Speaks: Being the Life Story of a Holy Man of the Oglala Sioux* (Lincoln: University of Nebraska Press, 2014),33.

PART TWO

EMBRACING LOVE

EACH LETTER IN THE WORD LOVE
REPRESENTS A SIGNIFICANT VALUE
THAT NURTURES THE ESSENCE OF LOVE.
LISTENING, OBSERVING, VALIDATING
AND EMPOWERING WHEN DONE WITH
LOVE ARE FREE OF JEALOUSY,
INSECURITY, EGO, AND CONTROL

CHAPTER FIVE

L = LISTENING

Nature has given us two ears, two eyes, and but one tongue - to the end that we should hear and see more than we speak.

Socrates

The first letter of the word love encompasses the essence of listening. From the place of the Good Wolf we listen to locate truth. We listen beneath and beyond false messages and fear. When we have located our Truth we arrive at clarity and from here will have a better idea of what to do.

> What separates and connects us more profoundly than miles, continents and economics are the messages we listen to and believe.

I had a dream recently where I experienced a great sense of relief when I located my Truth. In this dream my True Self listened to and observed my insecure False Self. I was in an uncomfortable situation. A woman whom I did not know was asking me questions about my life. She would ask her question in a pleasant tone, but each time I answered her, she replied with a statement that felt confusing and manipulative. In spite of this, I felt compelled to answer her questions with honesty. But each time I did, I felt like I was giving a sacred part of me away to her. As her questions persisted, she seemed to be gaining strength in a dominant and controlling way, and I seemed to be getting weaker. When I woke I wrote as many of the questions I could remember down.

> Lady: What are you doing?
>
> Me: Oh . . . I'm just writing.
>
> Lady: What are you writing about?
>
> Me: Oh . . . just random thoughts; I like to write
>
> Lady (with a sarcastic tone): OK, you're telling me you like to sit by yourself and write random thoughts?

Me (feeling guarded): Yes, I like this.

Lady: Do your friends think you're weird?

It felt to me that this dream lady's only purpose in eliciting information was to engage me and then attack me. I had piqued her interest, but she could not accept something she could not understand and felt justified in her negative attitudes towards me. The distress ended when my True Self, who was observing the situation, gave me some insight on what was happening. I was being guided by fear messages and was not listening to my true feelings which were informing me that I should not stay engaged in this unhealthy dynamic. By staying, I was feeding my Bad Wolf. I thought I had to answer this lady's questions even though they were not healthy for me. I took her comments personally and internalized them as injury.

As I stepped back into Self, I recognized the dynamic from this dream in past waking life experiences. I was driven by a fear of being admonished for not giving others what they needed or wanted from me. This dream helped me to recognize that this fear still existed within me on some levels. This awareness helped me feel calmer. Instead of waking up with lingering anxiety from a nightmare, I woke up feeling empowered with clarity.

The respected Swiss psychiatrist Carl Jung (1875 - 1961) validated this truth for me in his statement:

> Everything that irritates us about others can lead us to an understanding of ourselves.[27]

There are times we need support to help us sort our false messages from our Truth. We may gain clarity through a combination of many things including theory, spiritualty, trusted relationships, inspirational stories, leisure activity, and therapy. All of these are relevant. The most important thing is that we engage with what we seek. There are times when I am not a good fit for clients who are referred to me for therapy. In this case it is important I help connect this client to a better therapeutic fit for them. It is not the words we hear as much as the connection we experience that awaken us to a deeper awareness of Self. This connection is what matters.

---

[27] Carl Jung and Aniela Jaffé, *Memories, Dreams, Reflections* (New York: Random House, 1965), 247.

When I begin therapy with clients it is important for me to express that the therapy room is a place of exploration, but the real therapy room is in our life where we apply new clarity that leads us to new experiences. In the room, we can work towards making fear messages transparent and our Truth seen, but there is no shortcut to the change we desire. It is through our new experiences while engaged in life with our Truth that we observe differences in our Self. We may bring our great struggles of resistance back to the therapy room to explore further, but there is no substitute for life experience. In time we will no longer need the therapy room to help us clarify the difference between fear messages and Truth. We will become our own therapist, challenging our Self to go deeper with each insecurity we face.

> When we allow our Self to be on an exploratory path in our own lives, working through false beliefs and insecurities we will continually arrive at new awareness and will become better at listening for Truth.

Instead of letting our insecurities control us through acts of defensiveness, control of others, or allowing our Self to be controlled by others, we will increasingly be motivated by our natural inclinations. Instead of dreading the obstacles we face in life, we will know there is much we will learn and unlearn from them. With this awareness, we will fear our struggles less.

When we awake to an internal voice that we may have previously ignored due to insecurities, ego, avoidance, and false truths, we become connected to the voice of Self, our Good Wolf. This is the deep voice from within that guides us towards health, joy and interconnectedness. True Self is not a script we practice, and it cannot necessarily be defined; it is a feeling we trust and follow. It connects us to others in the natural way of the world where beautiful qualities of our true essence touch the true essence of others and life around us. It brings us out of the trappings of our mind and into our world. This is why we listen to the whisper of the Good Wolf.

Listening for Truth

> *When I do good, I feel good. When I do bad, I feel bad.*
> *That's my religion.*
> Abraham Lincoln

The moments in our lives where we experience love without conditions are the moments our True Self is embraced. These are cherished moments because they affirm what we know deep down but may not have always seen under the clutter of False Self's insecure messages and attachments.

Why else other than insecurity would we accept being treated badly and then go back for more? Why, other than because we are following false truths, would we dismiss kindred connections as insignificant? Sometimes we lose beautiful connections, not because they were not kindred to our Truth, but because we dismissed our Truth and closed a door to our beautiful Self.

We are all unique in our special needs for growth. What connects us is not just the interests we have in common but the respect we share for each other's uniqueness and the desire for happiness. My deepest relationships are ones built on mutual respect and the kindred desire to feed the Good Wolf. If we are judging others negatively because they have different interests, needs, and desires we will be closing our Self off to some pretty amazing new experiences. Worse, a negative comment and judgment from us can cause great harm to another who may be struggling with a fragile sense of Self.

Our words and attitudes can have a catastrophic impact on others; they can also have an immense positive impact. It is up to us to decide how to express them. We can break bad habits. We can learn better coping techniques. We can accept things that are different and enrich our life in the process. We find the most amazing friends in the most unlikely of places.

I had a wonderful experience last year that reminded me of the importance of listening to my Truth, not my fear. I had read a beautiful little book called *The Hen Who Dreamed She Could Fly* by Sun-mi Hwang.[28] In this story, a barnyard hen was born destined to a life of being locked in a chicken coop for the sole purpose of producing eggs. She allowed herself to dream of a life beyond the coop where one day she could keep her egg and nurture it to life. As fate would have it, she escaped the coop. She became stronger. She befriended a barnyard duck and nursed the egg of his wife who was killed by a weasel. Later her friend met this same fate, and she raised his son as her own. She followed her dreams and allowed her adopted son to follow his dreams, even when this meant he would leave the pond to live amongst wild ducks. She lived a full and happy life.

---

[28] Sun-Mi Hwang, *The Hen Who Dreamed She Could Fly: A Novel* (New York: Penguin, 2013).

A few months after reading this beautiful book, I met Henry the Barnyard Goose. Meeting Henry was a gift I shall forever treasure. I spotted Henry immediately amongst his adopted wild Canada Goose family. He was much bigger than his clan members, with a thick straight neck and a huge white chest he puffed out with pride. His beak was pink, thick and protruded straight out. He stood at the edge of his clan, giving no indication he did not belong there as he spread his wings wide and sunned his fat white belly. While I sat in awe of the wonder before me, I took out my notebook and wrote a little story that I later shared with my family and friends along with several pictures of Henry amongst his family:

Henry

This is a story about Henry. He is a domesticated barnyard goose. I met him yesterday. I am sure Henry has an amazing story of how he came to escape and fly free with his newly adopted wild family of Canada Geese. Henry is one of the happiest birds I have ever seen. In the way we feel when we are around someone happy - this is how I felt around Henry. He was so playful in his bliss. There was not one moment in the time I sat watching Henry that he was not embracing the wonders around him. Somehow Henry had found his way out of the barn and into the world. It was clear Henry was accepted by his new family. Two other Canada Goose families flew away when I approached the spot on the river where they were sunbathing, but Henry's clan did not fly. They seemed calm and at ease in their surroundings. When a speedboat came zipping by, the clan was startled and flew off. Just like the young duck in the book *The Hen Who Dreamed She Could Fly*, Henry took his position at the back of the V-shaped flying formation of his clan - the most vulnerable position to predators from behind. Perhaps Henry's presence gave his clan more confidence, and being adopted by this clan has assured Henry's survival in the wild. I felt so blessed meeting Henry. As he flew off with his head pushed forward and his wings flapping twice as hard to keep up to the others, I waved farewell and called up to him, "fly safe and soar free dear Henry, you are beautiful and so is your family."

I wondered how it was that Henry came to be with this family. In the area where I live, there are many small farms in which Canada Geese stop by on their regular rounds of foraging. I think Henry would have been a young gosling when he was adopted by this clan, as his primary wing feathers had not been clipped. Beginning at age seventeen weeks domesticated geese usually have their wing feathers clipped every year to keep them from flying off and discovering their Truth. Henry was living his Truth.

Even in the most extreme of situations, our True Self has never left. It may be buried below many false messages deeply yearning to be heard, but it has never left.

Listening for Meaningful Moments

> *What we have once enjoyed we can never lose. All that we love deeply becomes a part of us.*
> Helen Keller

It seems that the less we fear negative reactions to our healthy choices, the less power there is in a negative projection. Instead, we become more alert; we listen for experiences that connect to our Truth and follow this path. The more we do this, the more we will remember meaningful experiences from our past that may have been suppressed by our distractions.

Our True Self has been collecting meaningful moments
to return to us as gifts when we are ready to receive them.
The more I realize the significance of this Truth, I find
my Self increasingly open to receive blessings from the
past, present and future.

One of the golden memories I deeply cherish occurred many
years ago when I was working with street youth with HIV. I
took one of the two young woman I worked with for a day of
fun at a local amusement park. I had immense empathy for
this young woman. She had been socialized on the mean
streets of Vancouver British Columbia since birth. This young
woman was only eighteen at the time I knew her, but she
seemed much older as her body was so tired and depleted from
many years of abuse she had endured and then subjected
herself to.

She was so excited to go out for a day of fun. We took the bus
and I observed her demeanor change when around strangers.
She became loud and obnoxious. She told all kinds of stories
meant for others to hear; that were at best highly exaggerated
but mostly not true. All the while I listened to her stories I
could sense that she was anxious. We had a wonderful day at
the park taking in the thrill rides and laughing at the pure joy

of it all. I was honored to be sharing this day with her. This was her day - her joy was all that mattered.

When we caught our bus home, a young man from one of my college classes came on. He recognized me immediately and came to sit beside us. Without question or judgment he accepted my young friend. We were three people enjoying a great time together, and nothing else mattered. When he got off at the stop before ours he wished my young friend a happy marriage to her millionaire fiancé and a wonderful honeymoon on her cruise around the world; these were the tales she entertained him with on our bus ride home. He stood on the sidewalk waiting for the bus to drive off and waved up to my young friend who was plastered at the window waving back to him. Both had big wide grins on their faces.

When I saw this young man in class the following week he greeted me with laughter and told me that was by far the best bus ride he had ever had.

Our True Self is experienced in virtues of compassion, acceptance, patience, perseverance and above all, love. It is worth the effort to live in this Truth - it is much more fulfilling than living our lives in resentment, judgment, envy, and anger.

Just because someone is different than us does not mean they are not worthy of love and acceptance. If we believe this and greet others with love and acceptance, our lives will become enriched by the new experiences we have welcomed.

By taking time for our Self each day to relax and come back to our True Self Garden (even if for just five minutes), we will nurture a space in which we can gain clarity. Our true desire is to listen to our Good Wolf, and we need to nurture this relationship every day in order to be accessible to it. When we step back into the river of our life, with all of its distractions, we will be reminded of the wolf we want to guide us.

> With the clarity of Truth, our boundaries are
> communicated in allegiance with our Good Wolf. They
> remind Self that we are listening and respect the Truth we
> have come to know. In this light, we do not assert our
> boundaries with the intent to change other people to our
> way of thinking.

Another golden moment I cherish deeply is an observation my husband shared recently about his own growth.

Early in my relationship with my husband I had unrealistic expectations of him. I believed he should be my emotional rock even when he could not be available to me in this way. I remember there were times I took it upon myself to explain to him how he could go about attending to these shortcomings and be a better husband.

I falsely believed it was my husband's duty to help me heal from the injuries of my own struggles. When I recognized that the journey of healing and learning needed to be mine, I began to see my husband more fully, as a separate emotional being. I began to observe my insecurities from the place of my own Truth and came to recognize that I could be too accommodating with others. I came to see that this insecurity was driven by a fear of others being unhappy or disappointed in me.

I also recognized that when others interpreted my insecurities as permission to be controlling, this is when I would push back, but this struggle was emotionally exhausting.

I had to allow others to be disappointed in me. I could not always accommodate others at the expense of my Self or my family. There were some people I did need to drift away from, and there were people with whom I flowed deeper into relationships.

With my husband, I noticed that the more I listened to my Self, the more he would open up to me on deeper levels. The less I needed to rely on him to carry me, the more accessible I was for him to share his emotions with me. I became a better listener to his Truth. A while back I was having a conversation with him about this. He had quite an interesting observation about his own journey of growth. This is how I remember his words:

> When I was a young boy I did not think of these kinds of problems - I just naturally migrated to my interests and

to the people who I liked. In school I had to learn how to work with people whom I was not always naturally inclined to be with, but I still mostly moved naturally. When I was in university I felt some resistance in becoming a role I was to play in life - a career man with a nine-to-five job for the rest of my life - but I knew resistance was futile. I had a family, and I had dreams for my family. In my career I focused on building it: my portfolio, my working relationships and so on. Now I look back and see that everything was necessary for my growth. I have a deeper appreciation for meaningful relationships in my life, I am thankful for the growth, both personal and professional in my career - and I am proud of my family. I feel I have been on an amazing adventure which is not over. I feel like I am a much wiser version of that young boy again naturally migrating towards the wonders of life.

The more we nurture our Truth and guide our Self in this direction, the more we will be walking with our Good Wolf. We will become better listeners because we are not preoccupied with our own and others' discontentment or False Self needs. Our most beautiful connections with others are those in which we celebrate each other without judgment, envy and disregard.

CHAPTER SIX

O = Observing

To photograph truthfully and effectively is to see beneath the surfaces and record the qualities of nature and humanity which live or are latent in all things.
Ansel Adams

From the place of the Good Wolf the second letter in the word love, observing, is looking beyond the distractions, fear, and clutter in our life and focusing on what really matters. Through observing we not only embrace the beauty in our life that surrounds us day and night, but we also catch our Bad Wolf and intervene so we can rise with our Good Wolf.

I was sitting on my back porch with my eight-year-old nephew last summer after an overnight visit. He was asking me all sorts of questions about life and shared with me many of his observations on this subject. On the table sat a number of rocks he had collected down at the creek the day before.

"Where do you think the rocks came from?" he asked me.

"Can you imagine how old these rocks are! Do you think people lived on this property five hundred years ago? I wonder if there was a kid like me who played with the same rocks five hundred years ago! Do you think kids were happy five hundred years ago?"

Many of his questions I could not answer, and we wrote them down to research later that day. In the meantime I became distracted by a row of ants emerging onto the table to investigate the remnants of our breakfast. I shifted away from our conversation and grabbed a napkin and proceeded to squish the pesky critters. As I was wrapping their corpses into the napkin to discard, I noticed my nephew had become silent. Still holding the now-balled-up napkin in my right fist, I met the eyes of my horrified nephew.

First there was a heavy silence, then a deep breath. He was trying to refrain from saying something, but could no longer contain his troubled thoughts.

"Imagine if someone killed you because you were in the way - would that be nice?"

I could tell he took a risk in confronting me in this way. It was not easy for him. I felt horrible.

"No, that would not be nice at all," I said.

Feeling more at ease to express himself, my nephew went on,

"How would the ants know they were not allowed to be on the table? They were just looking for food. What if they had babies they needed to feed, and now they can't get back to them because you killed them?"

"You are right. I was not thinking about this; thank you for pointing this out. Next time I will move the ants without killing them."

I grabbed my notepad.

"Honey, I am going to write what you said down because it is an important message for everyone to hear."

Somewhat surprised he said,

"You mean even adults would listen?"

"Yes, of course. I am an adult, and you reminded me of an important lesson: that even the smallest of creatures deserve respect. Thank you very much for this lesson."

With this response my nephew had a grin from ear to ear, and his eyes twinkled with pride. I had affirmed his Truth . . . one of many he will come to know throughout his lifetime. Through standing up for what he believed, even to an adult, my eight-year-old nephew revealed a False Truth - that adults could not learn from children.

From Observation to Action

> *It is under the greatest adversity that there exists the greatest potential for doing good, both for oneself and others.*
> Dalai Lama XIV

There are times we observe a situation that escalates to the point where we feel the need to take action. We can no longer tolerate observing or participating in an activity that is causing our Self or others harm.

Sometimes we struggle with not being sure if we should take action, and later we come to regret this choice. These internal observations help to inform us in the future. The next time we come across a similar situation we will be more likely to move through fear and take action.

For example, we may observe someone being bullied and become aware to the potential for harm. Depending on whether we use the Good or Bad Wolf's eyes to observe, our response could be quite different. Following the example, we may observe that the bully, now feeling more confident in a position of dominance, begins to escalate as they feel they are gaining power over the increasingly distressed target of the bullying. When the situation escalates to this point, it is likely that everyone present is aware of it. At this point some observers may leave to avoid further involvement. Others may find a cathartic release of their own feelings of inferiority and collude with the bully so that they too can feel powerful. Finally, there are those who will not leave and do not tolerate such abusive behavior. They intervene, addressing the situation through Truth, not abuse. Their allegiance is to the Good Wolf.

It is likely we have all at one time or another been in the position of attacker, receiver, or avoider but have come to know that what supersedes insecurity is our desire to not cause harm. People who feel the need to control other people generally feel inadequate. If we nurture such insecurity, we will feed our Bad Wolf and seek submissiveness as a desirable trait to connect to in others.

If we feel we are being targeted by a negative dynamic, it is important to remind our Self that the negativity is coming from outside of us. We give it power if we internalize the projection by taking it personally. Instead, we can redirect our energy toward clarifying our Truth and guiding our Self from there. We can communicate from the place of our Truth much more clearly than from our fear. In fact, clarifying our Truth can be a wonderful reminder that our Self is strong, intact, and cannot be controlled. When we do not adopt an act of aggression by seeking to retaliate, we liberate our Self from attaching to insecurity. We do not accept an invitation to engage in a game that our Self has no desire to play.

As we work out of the clutches of our fears, we find our Self less preoccupied with judging or worrying about being judged by others. The dynamics that we once thought had control of us are now transparent and without power. As we continue to be guided by our Good Wolf, our life becomes more about how we live in our Truth and what we can offer to others to help them become accessible to their Truth. A quote by Thomas Paine (February 9, 1737 - June 8, 1809) an English and American political activist, philosopher, revolutionary and political theorist highlights this wisdom:

> He that would make his own liberty secure must guard even his enemy from oppression, for if he violates this duty, he establishes a precedent that will reach to himself.[29]

No one needs to accept mistreatment by another. Mistreatment feels terribly wrong because it is terribly wrong. This is why it is also wrong to retaliate with the same negative behaviors we are so against in others. There is no rationalization, no matter how institutionalized or believed,

---

[29] Thomas Paine, *Dissertations on First Principles of Government* (July 7, 1795), The Thomas Paine National Historical Association, accessed July 24, 2015, http://www.thomaspaine.org/major-works/dissertation-on-the-first-principles-of-government.html.

that justifies treating others differently than what we desire for our Self. We may find our Self up against some immensely powerful resistance to this Truth, but when we have been enlightened to it, we know that nothing can change it.

> When we see Truth we will never forget it; it becomes a part of our knowing.

We can all cause harm. The more curious we are about the ways we cause harm, the more transparent our actions become to us. As we open our Self up to this awareness, many things will be revealed to us over our lifetime which will bring us deeper into our relationship with our Self and others. Enlightenment to this truth has been a major catalyst in changing laws and the course of history. Our social laws were developed by us, and they can be rewritten by us. This is the power of our Truth. This is beautiful.

There is no story more compelling I can think of that highlights this awareness than the story of John Henry Newton.

John Henry Newton was born in England in the year 1725 and died in 1807. He is the man who wrote the powerful hymn

"Amazing Grace." His hymn penetrates through all False Self layers and strikes at the core of Truth where we can see it, feel it, and rejoice in it. For over two hundred years people all over the world have sung this beautiful song. It is an eternal gift. "Amazing Grace" embraces Truth, forgiveness and the everlasting light of love. I do not know a single person who is not aware of this hymn and is not moved by it.

As a young man barely out of adolescence, John Henry Newton worked on a slave ship that captured beautiful people of all ages from their homeland in Africa and forced them into slavery in distant lands. While on a voyage back to England from Africa around 1748, the ship Newton was working on nearly capsized in a horrible storm. Newton began to pray, and in this moment of clarity he began to see the truth of the human suffering he could no longer deny.

Miraculously the ship drifted to safety, and all on board survived. But John did not forget the Truth he touched. He marked the above event as the beginning of his journey to salvation. He did, however, remain involved in the slave trade, making three more voyages to Africa. He stopped his active involvement in slave trading in 1754 but remained involved by investing money in a slave trading company. The capturing and selling of people was a lucrative business. In time he could no longer rationalize his selfish gains at the expense of human lives, and by 1788 Newton had become an abolitionist.

John Henry Newton became passionate about appealing to the Truth in others on the issue of slavery. He wrote a powerful pamphlet called "Thoughts about the Slave Trade;" in it he described the horrific conditions on the ships and the treatment of the captured people. No one could argue with him as he spoke the truth about what he had been involved in and observed.

Newton also apologized profusely for his involvement in the slave trade with the following statement:

> . . . a confession, which comes too late . . . It will always be a subject of humiliating reflection to me, that I was once an active instrument in a business at which my heart now shudders.[30]

This pamphlet was so well received, it was difficult to keep up with print production. Having identified himself as a

---

[30] Adam Hochschild, *Bury the Chains: The British Struggle to Abolish Slavery* (New York: Houghton Mifflin Co. , 2005), 131.

Christian man who became a minister around 1757 and a priest in 1764, Newton said later in his life when he was an active abolitionist:

> I was greatly deficient in many respects. . . . I cannot consider myself to have been a believer in the full sense of the word, until a considerable time later.[31]

By finding and speaking his Truth, John Henry Newton made a profound and positive difference to the lives of many. In Newton's words:

> Amazing grace how sweet the sound, that saved a wretch like me.
> I once was lost but now am found.
> Was blind but now I see.

No matter how difficult the hours of struggle with our Truth may be, it is better for our Self and others to face that struggle. As the journey of John Henry Newton reveals, the difference each person's choices could make to the lives of many is far greater than the anguish and humility of one.

---

[31] John Newton, *Out of the Depths*, ed. Dennis R. Hillman (Grand Rapids: Kregel, 2003), 84.

It is love that takes us out of the confines of bitterness and ego and lifts us right up outside of our False Self into a world full of possibilities.

Being Accountable

> *Don't worry that children never listen to you; worry that they are always watching you.*
> Robert Fulghum

When we raise our young, we teach them that there are consequences for our actions. We teach them that they can hurt others with their actions and that they can make a positive difference with their actions. If we do not guide our Self with this same wisdom, our moral teachings will become a shallow representation of Truth.

When our loving words are congruent with our actions, the wisdom associated with them will resonate on deeper levels because they touch Truth.

A few years ago I had taken a friend's children out for a day of fun. The girl was eleven and the boy nine. We were pressed for time, but my car needed gas. Eagerly they jumped out of the car to take over the pumping, which prolonged this task considerably. While this was happening there was a woman making her way through the aisles of gas pumpers asking for money for a coffee. I observed people turning their heads away from her or simply saying no. She did not persist but made her way from one person to the next until she finally arrived at us. By now the kids had noticed her too and fell silent as she approached me. She looked exhausted and physically depleted, most likely from years of drug abuse compounded with not sleeping all night. Her male friend was sitting off to the side of the gas station and looked to be worse off than she. She could have been older or younger than me; I could not tell. In a hoarse, desperate voice she said,

"I don't want money; please when you go in to pay, can you buy me one large coffee?"

She was not asking for her friend, but I knew her intent was to share the coffee with him. Her eyes were pleading into my eyes. The kid's eyes were intently focused on me too. They were frightened and looked toward me for guidance. Amongst all the intensity there was clarity. I saw the woman's look of shame and felt empathy for her, not pity. She seemed to understand this and became calmer. The kids relaxed too.

"Yes," I replied to her,

"Why don't you go and get your coffee ready? I will pay for it when I'm done here."

There was no big show of gratitude nor did there need to be. This was understood. The kids understood too and quietly and observantly followed me into the gas station. I immediately informed the anxious-looking attendant that I was paying for the coffee and the woman piped in,

"I told you she was."

She was busy pouring as many creamers as she could into her large coffee, and I knew instantly she was hungry. To my left there was a section of ready-made sandwiches, and I discretely whispered to the kids to grab me a couple, which they did. I bought them, and as we were leaving handed them to the woman. She met my eyes with the same knowing gaze and said thank you. I nodded and left. The kids understood that day that we do need to be cautious when we are scared, but we do not need to be cruel. The Truth of others that day far superseded my need to rush.

The kids and their desire to have a new experience of pumping gas reminded me that when I slow down and observe what is happening around me I am better able to live in the essence of my Truth.

An exercise that reminds me to walk with my Good Wolf is reflecting on the values of my *ideal parent*. These are the values I believe would best guide me towards being a well-balanced person. I bring this exercise into the therapy room with my clients sometimes, and it never ceases to amaze me how consistent the values are. I simply ask,

"Imagine the parenting values that you feel would be ideal in raising you."

I encourage my clients to take as much time as needed to reflect on this question. Then I write down their observations and present them back as their own wisdom for guiding and nurturing themselves.

Here are some consistent observations of an ideal parent:

- being a good listener
- forgiving
- helping me to understand what I have done wrong without anger, rage, or ridicule
- caring
- loving
- patient
- available
- showing me that I matter by being there for me
- encouraging my strengths
- being assertive with me and others when needed
- not letting me get away with things that are not good for me
- having a positive outlook
- being consistent
- being a good example
- taking care of themselves so they can take care of their children

When these values are presented back to us as our own guiding wisdom they sound like this:

- I need to be a good listener to my Self
- I need to be forgiving with my Self and others

- I need to help my Self understand when I have done wrong without being angry, aggressive or negative towards my Self or others
- I need to be loving, patient and available to my Self
- I need to remind my Self that I matter and that I need to be there for my Self
- I need to encourage my strengths
- I need to be assertive with my Self and others sometimes
- I don't want to get away with things that are not good for me
- I want to nurture a positive outlook
- I want to be consistent
- I want to be a good example to my Self and others
- I want to take good care of my Self so I can be there in the ways I can for others

The reminders of history affirm that guiding our Self with love is the path to freedom. The examples are numerous: Nelson Mandela, amongst many South Africans, stood up and refused to accept apartheid and oppression; non-Jewish families living under Hitler's Nazi regime hid their Jewish neighbors in spite of meeting the same fate if they were caught; Rwandan Hutu citizens hid their Tutsi neighbors during the 1994 genocide;

the list can fill endless volumes of books. Each day there are beautiful people in our world who in spite of the threat of admonishment, stay true to their Good Wolf path. One of the worst injustices we can do to our Self and others is to nurture a stronger False Self to defend against another's False Self. As difficult as it can be at times to follow our path of Truth, we will feel internally grateful that we did.

CHAPTER SEVEN

V = VALIDATING

There are many truths of which the full meaning cannot be realized until personal experience has brought it home.

John Stuart Mill

The third letter in the word love represents validation which is an affirmation of our Truth - all that is good and loving about our Self and others. The feelings we recognize in light of our Truth are the feelings which will guide us. We will know we have strayed away from our Self when we are not in touch with these feelings.

When we recognize imbalance, we have an opportunity to look within and expose false truths and insecurities. Deep rooted false truths can feel extremely powerful, and if we do not make them transparent they will control us through our own defense of them.

When we recognize that our defense of false truths is a great fortress we build around our Self, our desire to live beyond these great walls of fear will far surpass the stones in our way. Our Good Wolf desires to take power away from the negative messages that feed our Bad Wolf. For example, if our experiences growing up taught us that we were not good enough or smart enough, we may be quite sensitive to criticism and may defend against injury from criticism by working hard to be smarter and better than others. In this case we falsely believe the effort to be better than others can protect our Self from feeling inadequate. What prompts us to see such false truth is recognizing that we are not being motivated from a secure or positive place.

With each negative feeling we identify and refrain from acting upon, we rise higher than insecurity and turn our attention back to our Truth.

Do we need others to notice us in order to feel affirmed? Do we treat others disrespectfully when we are stressed or tired? Do we listen to others in the same way we like others to listen to us? Do we tell our Self and others we are one thing, but we do another? Do we make excuses for our behaviors? Do we say "yes" when we want to say "no?" Do we need others to agree with us? Do we give our power to the person we perceive to be powerful? Do we think about the harm we cause our Self and others when we listen to these messages? When these questions matter more to us than the insecurity that drives them, we take power away from the Bad Wolf by changing the direction of our actions toward not causing harm. When we change direction, our experiences feel more authentic, balanced and fulfilling.

Being with our Truth opens us up to receiving the beautiful gifts around us; these gifts include connecting to the goodness in others. I am reminded of an event two years ago that validated the wonderful feeling I have when I am in the company of Good Wolves.

Like many reminders of Truth, this one occurred completely by surprise. My husband and I had traveled to Hawaii to attend my niece's wedding. She and her fiancé wanted a small, intimate wedding. The gathering included the bride and groom to be, her parents (including her stepmother), her fiancé's parents, myself, my husband, and an old family friend. It was a beautiful wedding on the beach at sunset. My sister (my niece's mother) stayed with us for a few nights after the wedding ceremonies at our rented condominium where we caught up on each other's lives.

Throughout the wedding festivities the whole group of us thoroughly enjoyed each other's company. Before everyone parted ways, my sister and I decided to invite the wedding party over for a barbeque at our place. My sister sent the invite out, but we did not hear back from anyone and assumed they were engaged with other activities. We thought nothing of this and went out for an adventuresome day of exploring. When we got back to the condo we decided a nap was in order. My husband went to the porch and I retreated to the bedroom; my sister collapsed on the pullout bed in the living room. I was awakened from a very contented nap by the noise of a crowd of very happy people inside our condo. The wedding party had arrived and were excited about their invite to dinner. Instead of being met with energetic greeting hosts, they were met by a sleeping host on a bed that consumed the living room. There was no evidence that dinner was on the agenda in this condo.

I scooped my hair into a bun, threw on a sundress and leaped out. I laughed at the sight of my beautiful sister scrambling off her bed as she was suddenly waked from her slumber by our excited guests; it seemed part of her destiny is to be in these sort of situations. I am laughing from the bottom of my heart as I remember this event. I think my sister shines at these unpredictable moments. She chose to stay dressed in her loungewear - why bother making a fuss now? was her attitude. For only a few seconds our excited guests hesitated, but this was fleeting. It was immediately apparent we were excited to see everybody and tumbled over in laughter at the whole mix-up. We stumbled over our words as we tried to explain, but it did not matter. We all enjoyed the irony of the moment - we invite everyone over for a celebratory dinner and then fall asleep. That is pretty funny. We knew this night was going to be fun.

Of course we had bought nothing to prepare for the dinner. Without question or hesitation our guests jumped to the occasion. My husband and my new nephew went shopping. My niece's father and her stepmother began getting things ready in the kitchen and took charge of the cooking. I was amazed at how everyone just jumped in so naturally. We had a fabulous time celebrating the newlyweds in an evening full of love.

What could have been an awkward moment turned out to be a memorable evening for all of us. It was apparent none of us wanted this evening to end. We all felt a uniting of families and told each other this before we parted ways. Not everyone responds to moments like this with such graciousness.

Some of the most memorable times in my life have been the spontaneous moments where we do not take life too seriously. We have freedom to see each other when we are not too fixed on our ideas of how life should be and how we should be in life. Sometimes we hesitate in a situation because we do not know how the other will respond to being caught off guard. We learn to be cautious of others' reactions until we understand more about how they will react. The dinner experience in Hawaii reminded me to not be too cautious of others' reactions when it comes at the expense of holding our beautiful Self back. Why not move in life with our True Self? This is how we get to know our Self and others more authentically. At any time we can decide if the path we are on is one we want to follow. In the meantime, we will be walking with our Truth and will open our Self to connecting to the Truth in others.

Locating Self

> *Consult not your fears but your hopes and dreams. Think not about your frustrations, but about your unfulfilled potential. Concern yourself not with what you tried and failed in, but with what it is still possible for you to do.*
> Pope John XXIII

We enter this world with a pure essence of Self, and we are naturally drawn to rediscover our Self. Sometimes we present a seedling that we want desperately to nourish, but our nurturers are sure it is a weed and they tell us to discard it. Perhaps we are a boy who wants to be a ballet dancer, but we are told this is wrong and are encouraged to play a sport we do not like. We still want to be a dancer, but every time we try to pursue this interest, the reaction from our nurturers is strong and we are told that our desire is wrong. The more we try, the more resistant our nurturers become. Finally we come to accept the false truth that if we are a boy, it is wrong to be a ballet dancer. We try hard to pursue the goals that others direct us toward, but they never seem to satisfy us. Our True Self still wants to be a dancer; we may find our Self pursuing this interest in secret and then feel ashamed for engaging in an interest we have learned is wrong.

In time there may be other negative messages attached to the first wrong message we received. We may wonder: What is wrong with me? I am a boy. I am not supposed to like ballet. When we are being punished consistently for the beautiful Self we are, the messages we learn are: I am not good enough. My ideas are stupid. Other people have better ideas than me. No matter what I do, I just can't seem to fit in. These are False Self messages that feed our Bad Wolf and bring weeds into our garden. When we learn that to be accepted is to be someone different than who we are, we will look outside of our Self for approval. But this approval by others will never feel good enough.

Imagine a different scenario for the boy who aspires to be a dancer. His parents may not have any desire themselves to be dancers, but they are curious and supportive about what interests their son. They see that their role is to nurture his interests and provide an environment for him to explore; in this way their world is also expanding.

Imagine this same young boy is now in school dancing for his friends in the schoolyard. He is seen by other children who have learned that "boys should not dance ballet," and they begin to ridicule and tease him. This experience may be devastating for this child, but he is fortunate to have mindful guides who have anticipated this and done their best to prepare their son for adversity. In this way negative experiences could be learning opportunities for their son to help him work through future adversity by not allowing the misguided beliefs of others to be incorporated into a False Self identify.

For people who have had chronically negative experiences growing up, locating True Self can be difficult. Finding empathy for people who are oppressed by other people is much easier than feeling empathy for those who harm others. If we respond to others' negative behaviors in a defensive way, we will be nurturing the False Self in both. We do not need to accept negative behaviors of others, but we can choose how we respond to them. Awareness that there is goodness in everyone, even if it is deeply buried under false truths, helps us to locate our compassion. This awareness helps us to practice patience and forgiveness with our Self and others and can open a door to empathy in ways we never imagined previously.

If our doors have been constantly closed and we come across an open one, why not take a chance and walk through it? We may discover the door we walked through was the passage to our life.

French born writer Victor Hugo's (1802 - 1885) famous book *Les Miserables* was published in 1862 and highlights the era between 1815 to 1835 Europe.[32] It is a beautiful story about the power of love, forgiveness, and giving others an opportunity for redemption. Hugo reminds us that, with a simple change of circumstances, we could all be walking in someone else's shoes. The main character in *Les Miserables*, Jean Valjean, is a peasant who served nineteen years in prison - five for stealing bread to feed his starving sister and her children, and fourteen for his numerous escape attempts. After release from prison Valjean cannot find a way to survive; he is constantly turned away because his yellow passport marks him as a former prisoner. A benevolent Bishop gives the desperate Valjean shelter. Tempted by opportunity, Valjean steals the Bishop's silverware. Valjean is captured by the police and denies he stole the silver, claiming it was given to him by the Bishop. Brought back to the Bishop with the stolen

---

[32] Victor Hugo, *Les Miserables* (Toronto: Penguin Books, 2012).

silver, the Bishop supports Valjean's story. In an effort to convince the police of Valjean's story, the Bishop hands Valjean two expensive silver candlesticks and tells him he had forgotten them the night before. When the police leave, the Bishop appeals to Valjean to use this wealth to make an honest man of himself. Although Valjean's past continues to haunt him, he does not forget the Bishop's generous gift of love. He turns his life around and feels compelled to live it with the same generosity and compassion that gave him the opportunity to save himself.

We should never feel guilty for growing, discovering and celebrating our beautiful Self; it is natural and should not be confused with egotistical motivations. When we strive with our Good Wolf to be the best person we can be we bring the gifts of our discoveries into the world and enrich our lives and the lives of others. If we allow our injuries and the misguided actions of others to suppress our beauty, we will push our Self behind a wall and deprive our Self and others of the beautiful gifts we have to offer. We can learn from the way others impact us - it informs us that our actions have a profound impact on others.

Reducing Harm

> *While the laughter of joy is in full harmony with our deeper life, the laughter of amusement should be kept apart from it. The danger is too great of thus learning to look at solemn things in a spirit of mockery, and to seek in them opportunities for exercising wit.*[33]
> Lewis Carrol

We can all cause harm. I have been guilty in my life of using negative humor at the expense of another, and I have been on the receiving end of it too. It is not pleasant. If the recipient is not enjoying humor at their expense, it is pretty much guaranteed we are not being funny for their amusement. We will know we are not taking responsibility for our actions if we say things like, "lighten up, I was just joking" or "you are being too sensitive." These statements do not validate the other's Truth, but they do strengthen our False Self.

We cannot underestimate how we impact the lives of others. If we take selfishly from others to satiate our desires, we will nurture emotional and physical gluttony at the expense of

---

[33] Lewis Carroll, *The Sayings of Lewis Carroll*, ed. Robert Peace (London: Derald Duckworth & Co., 1996) 51.

others. If we defend, deny or rationalize the negative impact of disregard, we will be an active participant in our own and others' oppression.

> When we reach beyond our Self it is not only our Self we rise with; that would be a lonely journey.

The so-called Golden Rule dates back to 551 - 479 BC in Confucian writing and is mentioned in all cultures around our world. The Golden Rule speaks to the need to think about others with compassion and respect. It asks that we treat others in the same manner we wish to be treated. The Golden Rule appeals to our Good Wolf and is commonly stated as:

Do unto others as you would have others do unto you.

When it matters to us that we do not cause harm, we nurture the essence of patience, forgiveness and Truth. Listening from our Truth will naturally come to us when we are driven to step out of the confines of our individual mind and connect to the true essence of others. We have so much to learn from others' experiences, thoughts, and dreams. If we shut others down to fill space with our own voice, we will isolate our Self to our mind and will miss an opportunity to open the door to experience others' beauty which is reflected back to them through us.

Validation from others helps us to locate our True Self. When this occurs, our awareness of Self expands and we can no longer deny that what we see is real. A dear friend of mine gave me a beautiful birthday card a few years ago that touched me deeply. Our desire for the other to be happy connects us like sisters. Here is the message from this beautiful card:

> We all let people into our lives, but you will find that really good friends let you into your own.[34]

Nurturing Meaningful Relationships

> *Keep away from people who try to belittle your ambitions. Small people always do that, but the really great people make you feel that you, too, can become great.*
>
> Mark Twain

---

[34] Leigh Standley, Curly Girl Design, accessed July 1, 2015, http://www.curlygirldesign.com

When my husband and I moved to a small town in the interior of British Columbia in 1983, I was in the first trimester of pregnancy with my first daughter. My husband had lived in this town previously and introduced me to a good friend of his. Without hesitation this young man welcomed me like a sister and so did his family. At this time in my life I was vulnerable, young, and pregnant and did not know anyone else in this town except my husband and his family. The unconditional acceptance of his friend was exactly what I needed. When we moved back to the big city two years later we became immersed with raising our family and furthering our studies. Our social life pretty much revolved around the university. A few years later our friend and his family uprooted from the interior and moved to another suburb of Vancouver. We maintained connection, but it was mostly around big events in each other's lives including his wedding to an amazing woman with whom he was perfectly matched in kindness and down-to-earth authenticity.

Our own lives were focused on events around school, career building, and raising children. There were times it felt too long between visits with our friends. When this happened, usually either one or the other would make contact. I do not think we fully realized back then that we were responding to our Truth when we listened to this desire. Without a doubt we realize this now. It is a gift to have kindred souls in our lives; they are worth making time for. We cherish the easy pleasure of being in each other's company. I know that this feeling is mutual, that we have grown into this knowing together. I am extremely grateful for this beautiful friendship.

We have obligations and distractions in our lives that can take us away from the time we want to spend with others; this is why our time is sacred. How we spend it can make all the difference.

> If we give too much of our Self to our insecurities, we will take precious time away from the most important relationships in our lives, which includes time with our Self. These relationships deserve our attention.

I love the time I spend with my family, dear friends and my Self. Sometimes I need more of one or the other. In our busy lives, it can be difficult to find leisure time with friends, but with every desire there is possibility, which leads to action.

Fourteen years ago I started a movie group that began with four of us and quickly morphed into a large group of thirteen woman. We call ourselves *The Movie Stars*, but now most us opt out of watching a movie and instead stay for an extended dinner catching up on each other's lives. We meet every second Wednesday after work and are all dear friends. We have been there for each other as we grieved significant losses, encouraged each other through periods of illness and adversity, rejoiced in each other's families, celebrated births and birthdays, retirements and accomplishments. We have found a way to keep connected amongst our busy lives because it matters to all of us that we do. One of the women touched the essence of our time with each other when she stated, "I love us." Not one of us take what we have for granted. We each have our own unique lives with various activities connected to it. It is unusual for all thirteen of us to be there at the same time, but knowing we have this time makes all the difference. This is why these gatherings work and are not taken for granted.

How we spend our time is a reflection of how we nurture our True Self. We have priorities that we will drop everything else for: our children, ailing loved ones, Self-care or a friend who is need of support. When people we care about are hurting, our True Self hurts too. Our love for others opens us up far beyond the boundaries of our physical knowing. When we embrace another in their pain, we feel empathy and a desire to help lift them. We animate a deep drive in our Self that takes us beyond our individual limitations and brings our relationships to a deeper level of trust and love. These are times we rise with the strength of the Good Wolf. In our efforts to help others access the strength of their Truth, we touch our own. "Look at this," our Good Wolf is saying; "Look at what really matters. Do you see your beauty? Isn't it wonderful?" Interestingly we experience a similar phenomenon when we embrace others' joy. When we are accessible to this love we are blessed.

Going on five years ago a devastating event happened in my life. My beautiful older sister died. She was forty-five years old. So young. So tired. So beautiful. I knew she was not well, but I was not prepared for such a loss. Even now, not one day goes by that I do not think of her. My father was married before and had two daughters from this union. A few years after his divorce, he left California for Canada with his second wife, my mother; this is where my sister, myself and my younger brother were born.

I did not grow up knowing my half- sisters who are eleven and ten years my senior. The eldest came to live with us for a year when I was very young but moved back to California, and there was no contact after that. I often fantasized about my California sisters, but I did not see them until I was an adult - and even then on only a few occasions. When my full sister died, I was devastated. I cry in this moment just thinking about her. Such a beautiful soul. My half- sister eleven years my senior, the younger of the two, reached out to me. She crashed through all barriers of time and distance. She had one purpose and that was to reach me and she did - right to the core of my heart. I knew without a doubt that she too had the same desire and longing over these years as I had - to connect with all of her sisters. She lost the opportunity on earth with one sister, and she was not going to lose it with the other. We are all children of the same father. Her love touched the core of mine and from here, the center of our awakened authentic Selves, we connect. My two eldest sisters and their beautiful daughters are all threads in my heart as my family is in theirs. From devastating loss came profound and lasting connection. It gives me great joy to believe this gift of love was orchestrated by our sister, now a soaring angel, forever solidifying our connections with the most eternal of bonds - love. After her death I came across one of her journals. There was a single entry - a quote of an Inuit legend that touches the essence of Good Wolf eternal love.

I who was born to die shall live. That the world of animals and the world of men may come together, I shall live.

When we nurture our Truth, we will be driven by a natural desire to validate the Truth we see in others in the hope that they too will see these qualities and rise with them. This is beautiful intent. Even if we were not exactly right on, our intent would still be beautiful - and it is this beauty that is the essence of Truth and is experienced by the other if they are open to it. When we rise with our own True Self, we will never forget this beauty.

> Accepting without judgment, forgiving without grudges, celebrating and loving without conditions give us space we need to see our Self and others and validate Truth.

Validation of our Truth not only helps us to manage negative projections from others; it helps us to keep our own negative thoughts in check so that we do not harm others. We will come to recognize that negative emotions such as anger, judgment, envy, and jealousy stop us from celebrating the joy of others. Negative emotions can keep others from wanting to celebrate their joy with us. Our Good Wolf desires to create opportunities for our Truth to be seen, not to shut it down.

CHAPTER EIGHT

E = EMPOWERING

I've come to believe that each of us has a personal calling that's as unique as a fingerprint - and that the best way to succeed is to discover what you love and then find a way to offer it to others in the form of service, working hard, and also allowing the energy of the universe to lead you.

Oprah Winfrey

The last letter in the word love, representing the word empowerment, is wonderfully placed. It encompasses the essence of listening, observing and validating. It is what we feel when we are walking proudly and strongly with our

Good Wolf in the world, and embracing and desiring the same feeling for others.

True Self-motivation arises from a deep yearning to exist in our world with love and to make a difference with this love. Where we feel compelled to go is our destiny. Empowerment is not *power over*; it is *power from within* - and it begins from deep within a nurtured True Self. There are many routes we take to access our Self, routes as various and unique as each person inhabiting this world. If we feel the routes we take in our life are better than the routes of others, we are not nurturing Good Wolf empowerment. Each of us have something unique and special to bring to this world, and our lives will become increasingly enriched by embracing this uniqueness. Others do not need to agree with our ideas; when we force ideas onto others we tend to push people away from us, not draw them closer. We do not need to travel another's path if it is not the right path for us. Good or bad - the choice is always ours. We all have choices.

Late fifth-century BC philosopher Socrates believed that choice was motivated by our desire for happiness. Wisdom, he believed, came from knowing oneself. The more we know our Self, the better our ability to reason and make choices based on our Truth. Socrates believed when we were guided by our Truth we would make better choices for the well-being of our society. [35]

Socrates was arrested, tried, convicted and sentenced to death by the Athenian democracy in 399 BC because his beliefs were felt to undermine state religion: he did not worship the gods the state worshipped. The other charge against him was that he was corrupting the minds of young people. In Plato's writing of his teacher in the letter *Apology*, he presents, as best he could, his understanding of why Socrates chose to stay in prison rather than deny his Truth to appease the discourse of the time. The speech Socrates offered in his own defense is the focus of Plato's *Apology*.[36] In his defense argument Socrates concludes that he has an awareness that his accusers lack: an open awareness of his own ignorance. Socrates refused to accept a sentence of exile from Athens and refused to commit to silence. Socrates maintained that "the unexamined life is not worth living for a human being," and

---

[35] Garth Kemerling, "Socrates: Philosophical Life," *Philosophy Pages*, last modified 12 November 2011, accessed May 15, 2015, http://www.philosophypages.com/hy/2d.htm.
[36] Debra Nails, "Socrates," in *The Stanford Encyclopedia of Philosophy* (Spring 2014 edition), ed. Edward N. Zalta, accessed July 1, 2015, http://plato.stanford.edu/archives/spr2014/entries/socrates/.

that he would rather die than give up philosophy. He was sentenced to death.

In his work *Crito*, Plato writes about Socrates' final days. He highlights a conversation between Socrates and his friend Crito. No matter the arguments Plato and others used to appeal to Socrates to escape the sentence of death, Socrates declined. Desperate to save Socrates' life, his friends appealed that other people will think his friends did not care enough about him to save him. Socrates retorts that what other people will say does not matter; that the only opinion that counts is from the one who truly knows, our Self. Socrates believed right up to the end, when he was sentenced to death by means of drinking poison hemlock, that it was this Truth that needed to be the basis of our human actions.[37] Just over two thousand four hundred years since Socrates death his Truth continues to prevail.

Nelson Mandela stood up to the oppressive South African Afrikaans National Party and for this he was imprisoned for twenty seven years; his Truth could not be suppressed. Lili'uokalani, the last queen of Hawaii, who in spite of severe oppressive and unjust charges designed to take what was left

---

[37] Kemerling, "Socrates."

of Hawaii away from its native people, held tight to her Truth and poured it into written word, lest it be forgotten.

We may not have to face the same degree of trials that these people did, but we will face trials that will challenge our Truth. Knowing these stories of great adversity and the power of love behind them give me strength to work through challenging times without losing my Self to fear.

> A well-nurtured True Self simply cannot betray Truth; there will never be peace in knowing we have betrayed the most sacred and eternal essence of our Self

I think we all like the idea of truth, but the question to our Self is, "are we living in our Truth?" We may study the language of truth and go to therapy or church to discover truth, but if we are not *living in our Truth,* we may run the risk of believing we have become a master of truth and not a humble student. There is a difference between sharing and claiming knowledge. Sharing is reciprocal; claiming is owning. We do not own knowledge. We will run the risk of feeling threatened by someone else's knowledge if we lay claim to knowledge. Do we deny the harm we cause others because we cannot tolerate the idea that we can cause harm? Do we turn conversations back to our Self when others are sharing? Do we remember other peoples' stories? Are we jealous of others' accomplishments? Do we need others to admire us for our knowledge and achievements? Our True Self beckons us to see the impact we have on others' lives. How we impact others' lives is how we impact our own life. Our True Self desires to work in the direction of connecting to others with love; this is naturally reflected in attributes of humbleness, forgiveness, and compassion. If we treat others and their stories dismissively, we will find they will not want to share themselves with us, and we will miss an opportunity to connect to their Truth. We will not be nurturing the true essence of our Self if we shut doors to others.

Often what we judge in others is a reflection of a false truth or insecurity we struggle with. This is important to recognize because negative judgments keep us separated, not connected. Maybe we want to dance in the rain and sing out loud like the person we are judging, but we fear what others would think. Perhaps we stop our Self from dancing in public because we have been negatively judged by another for embracing joy in this way. Perhaps we judge another when they share a vulnerability because we learned that to feel vulnerable is a character weakness. When we recognize the above dynamics are projections of our own insecurities and false truths we will be more inclined to want to work through our fears and false messages so we can be more accessible to our Self and others. Liberation from our fear can inspire others to be liberated from theirs too. Who doesn't desire to sing out loud, dance in the rain and not be closed off to exploring the wonders of life?

This image brings up a golden memory that touches the essence of living in my Truth. It was the summer I turned twenty-nine. A friend of mine and I were inspired to go on an adventure. We were going to go to Victoria, the capital of British Columbia on Vancouver Island, for two days - alone. We had a plan to take in the touring Genghis Khan exhibition at the Royal BC Museum in the heart of downtown Victoria but otherwise our time was free - ours to do whatever inspired us. Even though we drove to the ferry boat, walked on and then took a bus on the other side right to the center of our destination, we brought our backpacking gear and wore our hiking boots - our adventure gear. Oh, the fun we had laying on our packs on the deck of the BC Ferry, soaking up the sun. We were west coast hippies for a weekend and were embracing every moment of it.

We tromped all around a very hot and very busy Victoria with our packs looking for accommodation. This was tourist season, and we had great difficulty finding a place. There was a very old and somewhat weathered looking hotel near the center of everything which was our last resort. After exhausting all other options we had no choice but to walk into that old hotel and inquire if there was a room available, which of course there was. My first question to the desk attendant was, "I just need to ask, are the sheets clean?" He looked at me with amusement and replied, "Of course." We checked in, and the room was actually quaint and pleasant which led me to think that my question about the sheets had been ridiculous.

Like two school girls, we eagerly threw our packs off and rushed out to tromp around town. At the end of our adventuresome day we were drawn to some beautiful music by a group of three (two women and a man) performing on the promenade at Victoria Harbor. We sat on the steps directly in front of the historic parliament building along with a few other bystanders to enjoy this music. After each song my friend and I expressed our joy by clapping and shouting out praise for the great music these talented artists were sharing with us.

Sometimes we felt so inspired we would get up and swing each other around like highland dancers. The laughter coming out of us was pure joy. As dusk emerged the ocean blew in a rain cloud. The crowd thinned, but we could not bring ourselves to leave and neither could the performers. Soon it was just us. Night had now fallen, and the group of three gifted musicians entertained us with a final song. I will never forget that song. It was a rendition of Van Morrison's "Brown Eyed Girl." I have never heard it sung so animated and beautiful as it was performed that evening. Drenched under the coastal shower, my friend and I felt amazingly alive as we danced through that song from beginning to end. It was our farewell gift. I feel like getting up right now and dancing around my house to this beautiful memory. Drenched with rain and in our bliss, we hugged the group of three beautiful souls before departing and thanked each other for this magical and memorable evening.

That evening we literally collapsed into our beds, and both had a deep and blissful sleep. After waking the next morning I lay in bed resting my head on my elbow talking to my friend in the bed next to mine. In mid-sentence I gasped in shock when I caught the horrible site of a large dark yellow stain on the sheet right beside where my head rested. My sheets were dirty! My friend could not stop laughing at this happening to me. Recently I had a visit with her, and this story came up. The joy this memory gave was well worth sleeping on dirty sheets. These shared experiences of joy are lasting because they are experienced in our Truth.

> We were not born with insecurities. They are learned.
> The unraveling of them opens us up to our destiny.

Opening up to Possibilities

You and I are essentially infinite choice makers. In every moment of our existence, we are in that field of all possibilities where we have access to an infinity of choices.

Deepak Chopra

Our life stories can have an effect that is far more powerful and beautiful than our fears. When we do not judge our stories negatively, we become open to learning from them, and we are also less likely to judge others. From this perspective, what we may have once perceived as disempowerment now becomes empowerment. We come to embrace stories, not dishonor them. Every experience good and bad can bring us deeper into our Truth and deeper into our relationships with others. Sometimes we feel compelled to share our stories if we feel they will make a positive difference in someone else's life. But mostly our stories are a part of our Truth that we walk with every day.

The joy I feel when I embrace a part of my history that I had previously suppressed out of fear of negative judgment never ceases to amaze me. I feel deep gratitude for the times in my life I have liberated my Self from fear. This is Good Wolf empowerment.

Just the other day I observed this feeling of immense joy connected to being liberated from fear. I was telling some dear friends of mine about the fabulous budgeting strategy that I learned when I was a teen mother. I was not being either sarcastic or ironic with myself, just stating the truth as it was,

"when I was a teen mother and really poor I learned a fabulous budgeting strategy and I have come back to using it."

With great enthusiasm I went on,

"I took the money I had to live on for the month and divided it between mason jars with labels for various expenses such as food, bus fare and so on."

It felt so beautiful paying homage to this time of my life. I learned so much working through adversity. Going back to early discoveries in my life feels like I am honoring them. It is a reminder of my roots - the foundation I built. I often rediscover my Self when I come back to these roots. This is beautiful. I know my joy was felt by my friends. One of my friends remembered his days at university where he too had budgeted in a similar way; he smiled as he reminisced. When we celebrate our experiences of growth we liberate our Self from the threat of real or imagined negative judgment. No wonder it feels so good.

> If I shut my Truth down, I shut my Self down - I don't want to do that!

Opening Doors

You will come to a place where the streets are not marked. Some windows are lighted. But mostly they're darked. A place you could sprain both your elbow and chin! Do you dare to stay out? Do you dare to go in? How much can you lose? How much can you win?
Dr. Seuss

Good Wolf empowerment drives us to open doors and walk through them. The fears we worked through that brought us to new experience help us to swing the door open to more experience.

How amazing it feels to anticipate the possibilities behind doors. Where we once shuddered in fear of opening a door to the unknown, we now run with excitement toward it. Is that a door I see? . . . I can't wait to discover the possibilities on the other side of it! Recognizing that our defense of fears keep us trapped behind closed doors compels us to continue to face them, work through them, and travel deeper into our life. What often woke me up to this realization was my need to be there for my children.

It is through my love for them that I faced some massive fears propelling me to go deeper into my Truth where I overcame these fears. Children are a blessing, and we have a great responsibility to them. If we are blocked with fears that consume space, we will not be available to the people we love in the way we desire to be. In order to be present in the lives of others we need to be present in our own lives. More than anything else my children woke me up to this truth.

My youngest daughter has always had a spirited and creative nature. I remember thinking when she was little that she could illicit two very opposite responses from adults: one was that she could draw people who were attracted to her outgoing and imaginative personality, and the other was that she could annoy people who were more inclined to believe that "children should be seen but not heard." She simply was a child who would not allow her nature to be suppressed. I observed that her personality shifted to being somewhat defiant when she was around people who were distant with her. As most parents could appreciate, her father and I struggled with balancing the dilemma of teaching her manners, while at the same time validating her experience of being dismissed.

When she was in grade three I attended a routine parent-teacher meeting where parents receive updates on their children's progress in school. My daughter also attended this meeting. Shortly after the meeting began, I could sense her teacher was building up to tell me something significant; she appeared to be posturing in a defensive stance. I listened as the teacher began to tell me about a meeting the day prior involving an issue that came up with my daughter. While this was happening I observed something I had never seen before. My daughter was withdrawing into herself looking ashamed and insecure. The meeting the day before, I learned, had to do with a Christmas present plan my daughter had organized with three of her friends. The plan was that they would draw each other's names and buy a ten-dollar Christmas present for the person they picked.

The mothers of these friends were actively involved in volunteering at the school. They had an issue with the above plan, and somehow the teacher became involved. I immediately became alerted to an imbalanced power dynamic, and I asked the teacher questions about how this objection came out.

I learned that the meeting involved all of the other mothers with the teacher and my daughter; these women expressed to my daughter their dislike of her plan because it put too much financial pressure on their children. The important details were not being offered so I asked,

"Was my daughter the only child present?"

The teacher confirmed that she was. My heart was in pain for my daughter. How horribly confusing and scary for her. Her plan had come from her heart. I remember how happy she was when she came home the week prior, telling me about this idea that she and her friends had come up with at lunch time.

I was devastated that my child had to go through such a traumatic experience. There was no adult present to support her. My heart wrenched knowing that she felt so ashamed of her plan that she did not tell me or her father of this horrible meeting the day before. I was feeling extremely angry over this situation and extremely sad and empathetic for my daughter. I could not keep my eyes off my daughter and felt a strong need to validate her. In that moment it was all that mattered. I said,

"Honey, this must have been horrible for you. I am so sorry you had to go through this."

I did not stop there and went on to tell her,

"Even though your plan did not work out, it came from your heart and that is not a bad thing."

My daughter's eyes lifted and met mine. When I was sure her beautiful spirit had returned, I turned to address her teacher. I experienced myself having to contain my anger, but I felt strong and clear in my position that what the teacher had allowed to happen was wrong. In a much different tone, I told my daughter's teacher in the way I wanted my daughter to hear,

"This meeting you had was wrong."

There was a brief silence, but it was clear the teacher's demeanor changed. I knew that she understood that what she had allowed to happen was wrong. She apologized to my daughter, and graciously my little girl accepted this apology.

I was deeply troubled by the events around this meeting, and I did ask myself how this could have happened without me knowing anything. I stepped back and took a long hard look at my own life. My husband and I were exceptionally young parents who were working hard at making a good future for our family; we were both attending full-time university at this time. In spite of this, we had time for our family, and our activities and friendships revolved around our family. We were on an adventure together. Up until this moment I really did not question my priorities as I thought they were balanced enough.

As I took a deeper look into my life, I recognized I had some negative experiences with being judged as a visibly young mother. I looked fourteen-years-old when I had my first daughter at eighteen, and I looked not much older when my second daughter was born eighteen months later. Our ages were not an issue with the people we knew, but in some settings where we were visible symbols of what others learned is wrong in our society, we did experience the stigma of negative judgment. It became quickly apparent that being the female, I was generally judged more harshly than my husband who was more often viewed sympathetically. Our daughter's elementary school was one of those places where these negative stereotypes existed. Consciously I began to tune out negative judgment, and I interacted with the school on an as needed basis, playing tag team with my husband in direct dealings with this school.

After the incident concerning my daughter, I realized that by "tuning out negativity" I also tuned out some significant events that revolved around my daughter. I grew wiser and stronger that dreadful day. Over time there were other moments in my daughters' lives where they needed us to advocate for them, and I knew they could trust that we would be available for them - not always with the outcome they may have had in mind, but with their best interest in mind. We were stumbling along as a family but what drove our growth was, and still is, a deep sense of love and care for each other.

Many of our lessons come from learning from our mistakes; because of this, we learn the power of forgiveness.

All of our experiences - including our struggles, celebrations and achievements - are a part of our life's journey and lead us down the path of our destiny. When we embrace experiences, we are open to learning from them. True Self-empowerment is a reflection of working through fears that block us from our Self and others, and it is experienced in the capacity we have for compassion and love.

To live in Truth is living our destiny. When our beautiful gifts are met with jealousy and behaviors designed to shut them down, this is only because the other has not touched their own beauty. Each of us has a destiny to follow, and we cannot do this if we are oppressed by fears. Our Good Wolf calls us to follow the path of our destiny where we celebrate our gifts and the gifts of others. Anything else is clutter we must find a way to move past.

The star that lights our torch is within all of us. We are the star. When we nurture our Truth, we keep our flame lit and walk with faith that it will guide us deeper into our destiny. As we go forth and offer our burning torch to unlit ones we meet along the way, we contribute to a cycle of life where newly lit torches can ignite others flames. A world where it is understood as naturally as breathing air, that our torch of Truth stays lit when it lights the torches of others - this is the utopia of the Good Wolf.

ACKNOWLEDGMENTS

I have been on a beautiful journey writing the *Rise of the Good Wolf.* What began as a desire to leave a legacy of love for my daughters became a profound reminder that love comes from our connections in the world and needs to be brought back into the world where it can reach others. In writing this book I was continually reminded that we are not on this journey alone. Each thread we connect to that brings us closer to our Truth also brings us deeper into our relationships with others. When we honor these relationships we are reminded of where our beautiful gifts come from - lest we forget.

There are people I have not met who have greatly impacted my life. Their love has influenced this story in profound ways. Their desire to help others rise with their Truth, even if this meant sacrificing their own freedom, is a legacy that reaches beyond time and borders.

Nelson Mandela (1918 - 2013) in memorandum, from the time I first learned of you when I was barely a woman, your journey has inspired me to step outside of myself and care for others in the world - I am eternally grateful for this. The power of your forgiveness is a legacy that will continue to touch others in our eternal web of life - your journey is a testament to the power of love.

Donald W. Winnicott (1896 - 1971) in memorandum, I cannot thank you enough for introducing me to the concepts of True Self and False Self. You presented these concepts in such a way that we can all be accessible to them as a part of our internal knowing. In a world full of immense distractions you gave us clarity to be guided with.

Anne Morrow Lindbergh (1906 - 2001) in memorandum, you have inspired me to rise with my Good Wolf. As thousands before me, I felt blessed when I came across your book *Gift from the Sea.* So often when I battled resistance to take time for my Self, I thought about your beautiful words and that was enough of a reminder to listen to my Truth and do what I needed to do. What I have learned about your life greatly humbles and inspires me. You are a precious gift Anne Morrow Lindbergh; a treasure for all those who are blessed to be touched by your love. Thank you.

Lili'uokalani (1838 - 1917) in memorandum, the gift you left for your people when you wrote for them *Hawai'i's Story by Hawai'i's Queen* is a gift you left for the world. We can all learn from your messages. Your story is a powerful reminder that nothing is worth the cost of ignoring Truth. As I write these words I am experiencing that same inner feeling of empowerment I experienced throughout reading your book of love. May the Truth of your people prevail!

Dr. David Heilbrunn, you are one the golden gifts I have received in my life. The psychodynamic skills you taught me over a span of eight years, early in my career as a therapist, inspired me to go deeper into my Truth; which enabled me to help others go deeper into their Truth. Many times throughout the journey of writing this book, I paused and gave thanks for the deeper knowing I have come to because of the doors you encouraged me to open. Thank you.

I am deeply grateful to Coleen Richey, Pamela Booker, Samantha Saffy, Terry Pellatt, Sharan Sandhu, David Kealy and Bonnie Kennedy for reading this manuscript at various stages of its development. The regard you gave to this story resonates through the pages of this book. Thank you for embracing the Good Wolf and thank you for your beautiful love.

The wonders of this journey expanded in ways I could not have previously imagined when I sought guidance from an editor. I will never forget my first meeting with Betsy Warland. With my first rough draft, you saw the *Good Wolf*. You saw the potential. You told me I had a book, and then then you told me I had some work to do. You opened me up to layers I needed to look at to bring the voice of the *Good Wolf* to light - especially bringing my Self into the story. Your belief in me that I could tell this story gave me inspiration to go deeper, where the *Good Wolf* could be fully realized. I thank you from the bottom of my heart for this. When you saw this had been achieved, you introduced me to Betsy Nuse to assist with bringing this work to finish.

Betsy Nuse is the embodiment of patience. I have received emails from Betsy which were sent a 5:00 a.m. I cannot thank you enough Betsy for your dedication to the work you do for others. When someone believes in us, we soar. Your invaluable editorial skills, patience and dedication have helped the *Good Wolf* soar. To have another embody your work with the intention to help you bring the soul of your work to light is a beautiful and generous gift. This is the gift I was given from the two amazing Betsy's.

My daughters Natashia and Shavaun. You, my precious angels, have always been the extra beat in my heart that has propelled me beyond the idea of limitations. From the day you were born, I knew there was something much higher than me to reach for. This book is just one more example of what we discover when we are inspired by our love for others. Thank you for your precious love.

My beautiful husband and partner through life, Marlow, what a journey we have been on. Sometimes I need to step back and remind myself that we were once two separate souls that did not yet know each other. Is that even possible? Thank you for always believing in me and thank you for believing in the Good Wolf. Thank you for your hours of gracious proofreading, and thank you for the years of beautiful memories and adventures. To think that we once joked about traveling in two different directions, you to the earth sciences, and me to the social sciences - only to come full circle in our realization that earth and humans are interconnected. No wonder we have always inspired each other.

I am deeply grateful to my father, Arthur Douglas Lafferty - your love of nature and your positive outlook on life is a profound legacy of love you have given to your family and to the many souls your life has touched. This story is just one of the many ways your love has inspired others in this beautiful world of ours. I promise to always leave the campsite cleaner than when I arrived.

There are so many beautiful people reflected on the pages of this book that have impacted my life - you are all part of the weave of experience that fuel destinies forward. Cherished family and dear friends - thank you for your love.

Through each person walking in this world with their Good Wolf, several thousand more will be touched. By the time we cycle through these threads we will have covered the world with this love. Without you this story could not have been possible.

ABOUT THE AUTHOR

Kelly Pellatt wanted to give back. This was the passion that drove her to go back to college and to find her first job working at a group home for teen mothers in government care in 1988 when she was barely into adulthood herself. From her own experience as a teen mother she felt she had much to offer other young mothers facing adversity. She believed that support and having someone 'believe in us' would make as profound a difference as it did for her. She did not anticipate that the majority of the population she would work with had entered the group home from a street entrenched life which compounded the adversities they faced. The hardships facing these young women led twenty-two year-old Kelly to venture deeper into her compassion for others. Working the night shift had its benefits, as this was a quiet time where the youth were more apt to sit down and share their deeper thoughts:

> I was captivated by their stories and their desire for a better life. I experienced a deep compassion and drive

to encourage them to follow their dreams which I innately felt would lead them to a better life for themselves and their young children.

It was while working with these teen mothers Kelly came to recognize a profound dynamic:

> It struck me that the more I saw and connected to their authentic Selves, the more frequently I would see these beautiful attributes beneath everything else - bad things did happen and many of them had their children apprehended by the government, but the seeds of their True Selves were seen and I believed they now had a focus to work on - I felt this to be profound; later I recognized how blessed I was to work for an agency which had a supportive and encouraging approach to these young women.

With the same agency, Kelly covered shifts at a home for teenagers with HIV and again found immense compassion for these young people facing colossal adversity.

> I really was not thinking about my future career in a structured way, I was just following a deeper desire

that was awakening in me to help others in whatever capacity my destiny took me.

After completing her Bachelor of Social Work degree in 1994, Kelly began work as a Youth and Family Worker and Alternate Program Worker with the Vancouver School Board where she worked with youth facing immense challenges.

> I saw adversity affecting so many lives in so many ways; I saw that in each situation these young people faced, any one of us could have experienced these things with a change of circumstances; what mattered most was that these kids had their beautiful qualities noticed underneath their adversity with the
> hope they would see them and rise with them.

Kelly decided to go back to university and pursue a career as a therapist working with adults. She completed her Master of Social Work degree in 1998 and since this time has been working full time as a therapist in adult mental health in Surrey, British Columbia, Canada.

> No matter our age and experiences, it is never too late to discover our beauty.

What began as a profound journey of rising in her Truth, led to a career in assisting others to locate their Truth.

Kelly Pellatt lives in Langley, British Columbia with her husband Marlow and German Shepherd Kulshan. She counts her blessings to have her daughters, Natashia, Shavaun, daughter-in-law Erin and grandson Hudson live close by. *Rise of the Good Wolf* is her first book.

Made in the USA
San Bernardino, CA
21 February 2016